The Seven Deadliest Words

The Power of Words:
The Power to Heal

Dr. Thomas L. Page

TRUE DIRECTIONS | **⊘iUniverse®**
AN AFFILIATE OF TARCHER PERIGEE

THE SEVEN
THE POWER OF WORDS: THE POWER TO HEAL

iUniverse books may be ordered through booksellers or by contacting:

iUniverse
1663 Liberty Drive
Bloomington, IN 47403
www.iuniverse.com
1-800-Authors (1-800-288-4677)

ISBN: 978-1-4917-8760-1 (sc)
ISBN: 978-1-4917-8759-5 (hc)
ISBN: 978-1-4917-8758-8 (e)

Library of Congress Control Number: 2016900888

Print information available on the last page.

iUniverse rev. date: 02/18/2016

"Ask, and it will be given to you; seek, and you will find; knock, and it will be opened to you."

[Matthew 7:7]

I asked God for a sign to help me with this book. He gave it to me. I listened to His voice as I kept still to listen. He opened my heart so that my ears can hear the words to inspire me. He gave me the vision to see the people that I needed to seek. And now, for my obedience to Him... it is through Him... that doors I knock on will now be opened for me.

Dr. Thomas L. Page

ACKNOWLEDGEMENTS

God is good. God is awesome. This book has finally come full circle. God has given me the vision for this book. I couldn't have done it without Him. This book has been on my heart, mind and spirit for a couple of years, but I kept putting off for many reasons. Finances was one of the excuses. I didn't want to lose any of the jobs I had in order to stay financially stable to survive. The truth was that I didn't trust myself enough to think that this book would take me far enough to keep me financially stable. I had built up a fear of failing ... so bad that I put the book away for a long time because I had given up on the notion that if my first book didn't reach the masses that I needed to get to, what would make this book any different?

Well, God had another plan for me and put specific people in my life when it came to this particular book. It's funny how God makes us listen at the time we need to the most. Momma and Pop, you have been the constant source that God has put into my life to make sure that you are never forgotten. You forever remain constant within my heart and soul. You are the ones who made me believe in myself when I had lost faith in myself, at a time in my journey where I'd thought I had given up on God and even the both of you. Your unconditional love sustained me. Your presence as a mother and father embraced me, kept me believing that I would be as great of a parent as you have been to me. The both of you always taught me that even though we were poor in the material sense, we had each other as a family. That was that richest gift I could have ever been given. God knew what He was doing when He gave me the both of you. Your legacy will live on. Because of the both of you, I know there is a God. Because of the both of you, I know that I am never alone in this world and on this journey. You have prepared me for this journey since birth. I hope that I have done you proud as a son. Know that this book will be a testimony to the both of you that anything can happen with the true support of those who love you and stand behind you … no matter what. Thank you, Momma and Pop.

Dr. Bob Lee, thank you for staying the course with me and helping me build a platform with my first book. God put you in my life to make sure that I didn't give up on my mission in life … spreading the message of God's love and mercy through my writing and messages that I have for others. It was because of you that I started my second book, again. You will never know the impact you had on my life when you gave me the opportunity to promote my first book on your show. You believed in my book. You believed that I had a message that was good enough to be told to the many who see your show. That was the first true sign that God gave me to start working on my second book and staying on this journey until completion, not really knowing the plans He has in store for me. He placed in my life a brother, a friend, and a supporter who has been a true inspiration and guiding force in this journey. I hope that you will always remain as that brother and friend and never stop being an inspiration to many as you have been for me.

Finally, to Steve Harvey. Thank you for your devotion in these last few months of me completing my book. I have never gotten up early enough to listen to the morning inspirational devotions you give. However, for some reason, I was awaken by the alarm and heard your music introduction. Instead of turning it off as I usually would do, I kept it on. You talked about the airplane and taking a leap of faith. I have taken that leap of faith that you mentioned. I've been listening ever since. I was especially touched by three of your morning devotions. There were three particular devotions that moved me to complete this book. Your words of inspiration when you talked about the elder of the church you met in your travels. You mentioned how this disciple of God had you realize that this was your time and how God is using you at this time. He reminded you that it wasn't your time before now because God prepared you for this particular time in your journey. You woke me up and talked to me that morning. My life was never the same since that message. You made me realize through your devotions that God had given me a wakeup call ... telling me (through your words of encouragement) that it was now my time and all I needed to do was write this book and let God do the rest.

Your devotion about your friend with his patents that he never did anything with, made me realize that I was that person. I was making excuses out of fear because of what I thought I didn't have to complete this book. So, I stopped working on it. Even though I didn't have the money and the resources necessary to make this happen for me, you slapped me in the face and reminded me that I had God's blessing to complete this book and to rely on prayer and faith that all things will work together for those who believe. Your words and devotion hit home and hit hard. I stopped making excuses and did what I was called to do because you screamed at me and made it loud and clear to me what God wanted me to do through your inspirational messages.

You got your radio show ... and now I finally got my second book completed because of your words from God. Thank you. Thank you. Thank you. I allowed it to happen as you suggested by letting God take over. You said that I was never alone in this journey. God and prayer has always been my life's purpose. I just had to slow down and return to the basics (prayer, faith, and hearing God's message and letting it work through me). I took that leap that you mentioned in the third devotional message that assured me this book was meant to happen. I don't know where this book is going to take me. All I know now is that this book is God inspired and written in honor to God for His people to let them know that they are not alone in this world. They can have the joy and momentum that you and I have found in our walk ... through God's GRACE and MERCY. Thank you for your morning devotional time. These last two months of my life has changed because God spoke to me through you and your morning devotional words.

I am no longer afraid to ask for help. I am no longer bound by excuses about writing this book, and I know for sure that I have truly listened to God and followed his steps in order for me to get to this moment in my journey. This is my time. This is my purpose that God has for me. And now, I stand with the hope and faith that I knew that I'd always had. It just took God's messenger to wake me up and say ... "It's time." Thank you, Steve Harvey for letting God use you once again. One day, I will meet you face to face to thank you, personally, for all you have done to get me to this place in my journey. You are truly one of God's messengers. Never stop your messages. Never stop believing. Prayer works.

"In the beginning was the Word, and the Word was with God, and the Word was God."
John 1: 1

"This is where it all begins and ends for me. It begins with God and will end with God."
Dr. Thomas L. Page

INTRODUCTION

This is where my next journey begins. It begins with God and will end with God.

This book is going to be dedicated to those who really want to change their lives and make a renewed dedication for themselves for the better. Sometimes all we have to do is look deep within ourselves, acknowledge our shortcomings in our lives, changes those shortcomings into possibilities and make a promise to ourselves to put that possibility into action in order to make that change happen.

For a long time now I have been taking the time to look at my own life and doing some serious soul searching in order for me to live the life that I desired and became successful at. It was not an easy journey at all. There were a lot of adversities that I had to go through. However, there were a lot of great accomplishments that I have reached that also helped me get to this point in life. When I look at my life now, I smile because I made the tough choices that had to be made, and survived the losses and made it through the storm called "life."

If I had to base my life on my present success, I would have to base it on the *seven deadliest words* that kept me from succeeding at first and how I learned to take those words and change my life completely, using them to my advantage. Now, you are probably saying what seven words could possibly be the deadliest words that could affect our lives that much that it would hold us back and stop us from living our most successful lives; yet, can move us forward and meet our desired goals to be the best person that we can be. There are many words that could hold us back and keep us from being the best person that we could be. But know that the same words that you think could hold you back, can be the very same words that change your life for the better.

This book is going to tell you about the seven words in my own personal life that changed me. Hopefully this book will help you come to a point in your life where you might want to change some things in your own life if you find yourself being stuck in situations you want to get out, but need some instructions on how to get to that place in your life in order to be the best you can be.

In order for this book to be of any help to you, there are a few things that you will need to know. First, these are my seven words that changed my life. These may not be your seven words. You may have seven other deadliest words in your life that you might want to create by the time you finish reading this book in order to enhance your life. You will have the opportunity to do that. Secondly, there will be some interactive exercises for you to complete, in the hope that it will help you find some possible strategies to help you accomplish your goal in becoming the best you can be.

This isn't going to be a book that is going to give you instant answers and instant success. The intent of this book is to help you acknowledge some of the weaknesses that may be holding you back and preventing you from growing physically, mentally, spiritually and emotionally, and help you to create some possible strategies to enhance those strengths you do have and continue to build on those strengths that you may find that were lacking in your personal growth in order to help you develop possibilities in becoming the best person you can be. Let's start with the first word.

"Commit your work to the Lord, and
your plans will be established."
Proverbs 16:3

"The success of any man is one who can stay committed
to his vision...while staying focused on **His** vision."
Dr. Thomas L. Page

"SUCCESS"

Before I share my journey of success with you, I would like for you to take at least a few moments to think about what success means to you and for you. When you think of *success*, what five words come to mind for you?

1. _____
2. _____
3. _____
4. _____
5. _____

I hope that you were able to come up with 5 words that came to mind when you thought of *success*. If you were not really able to come up with 5 words, see if you can complete this sentence:

"I measure my success by

_____

_____

_____

_____

_____."

How did you do? Were you able to come up with five words or a complete sentence? If you weren't able to, you are not alone in this struggle. All of us at some point have had (and still have) issues on what *success* is. Even more so, many are struggling to know if they would consider themselves a *success*. How about you?

For a long time, I'd always thought success was having the best of everything. *Success* was no longer being poor, making sure that when I grew up, I would complete my educational path, the employment path, and making sure that I made more than enough money to take care of my family, parents, brothers, sisters, and those who couldn't help themselves. I would imagine *success* to be living in that mansion on top of the hill and having that home in the Hamptons and a winter vacation home to get away whenever I wanted to. *Success* was not having to work anymore. Having the luxuries of the world that I couldn't afford when I was a child growing up into the adolescent phase was all I wanted. I wanted all the clothes and shoes that I could fit in the biggest closet I could build. I would imagine success (at the time) being on the cover of GQ or Esquire and meeting the status of richness that I longed for in fashion. It wasn't just being comfortable … it was about having it all. I measured *success* by what I saw on television, watching shows that would fill my head up with so many dreams and wishes I couldn't even hold it all in. I would imagine being one of the Carringtons in "Dynasty.'" I would imagine playing the part of Dominique Devereaux's missing son. I would even dream while watching television at being a rich oil tycoon like the Ewings in the show "Dallas." Anything that television deemed as success, that is what I wanted.

The funny thing about that type of success was that it didn't work for me. My eyes were on the wrong prize. Everything I knew about success was not in the right context. Everything about success (at that time), focused on the material things that I knew I couldn't have at the time and the dreams I couldn't fulfill because I would daydream so much, I missed the most important times of my life and let those moments I really needed to make those possibilities happen in my life pass me by.

I would take the wrong opportunities thinking that if I did the quick, get rich opportunities, I wouldn't have to work another day. It seemed as though that I had done everything in order to make my life richer. I had thought of becoming an undercover drug dealer because they made the fast, easy money that wasn't taxed. I had even thought of becoming a stripper because of the great tips and the fast money that was being made by some of my friends that were doing it. All through these thoughts I was having, I kept asking myself … "What am I doing wrong?" "What am I missing in my life that I can't make this money and become a success?" The biggest question that I finally asked myself was, "Why is God punishing me for doing the right things that don't seem to work?" I thought I was doing everything right and by the book. I would go to church and follow the teachings of the "Word." I would say to myself that maybe this was just a phase … feeling sorry for myself and would get through it and God would bless me with the riches I desired to be a success.

Wanting to be a success almost killed me. I kept saying to myself that if I worked enough jobs that I would make the money I would need to be a success. I would do the noble thing and just work. I found myself working three to four jobs trying to make the money I needed to be a success. I ended up in the hospital with a bad case of ulcers in my twenties. Had migraine headaches so bad that I couldn't lift my head off of the pillow in my thirties. Now, even though I never thought of suicide as an option, I thought of giving up and walking away from the little bit that I did have.

It was at that moment where I got a break from God (or what I thought was a break from God), where I was going to become the success I desired to be. I was offered a job in Houston, Texas where I worked my butt off. I'd finally made the money I truly wanted to make and I had a great home and everything I thought I needed to be a success. Then, the stocks crashed. It was during the time of the big stock crash that it seemed that most of the workers in Houston lost their jobs. I happened to have been one of them that lost that great job. I didn't think at the time that this could happen to me. This was *success* for me. Things were going really well and I had finally found the *success* that I truly wanted and needed in my life. At least I thought I did.

As time went on, I couldn't find any jobs and times were getting tough. I couldn't go back home to New Jersey. I wouldn't go back home to New Jersey. My parents were really proud of me at that time and telling them that I had lost my job and telling them of the struggles that I was going through would have been seen to me as being a failure. My parents had already lost a son to drugs and they went through enough struggles in their own lives and I didn't want to put any additional burdens on them to ask for help. So, I stayed in Houston, sold most of the things that I had to survive, lost the place where I was living, and found myself homeless. I was living from day to day, not knowing where to go, and most of the time I was hungry, but too proud to beg for food to eat. I would look for jobs, but there were none. In spite of it all, I lost the *success* that I thought was the *"be all to end all."* At that time, everything I lived for and worked for seemed to had gone downhill for me and I really just wanted to have someplace to rest my head and a place to eat. I had forgotten all about *success*. All I knew was that at the time, *success* was nowhere to be found.

This is the point where I truly believed that God had given up on me. Even though I thought my intentions were good by doing the "right" things in my life, I thought God left me alone in the world to fend for myself because I had turned my back on Him and went my own way and did my own thing. No matter how much I kept praying, I felt that God was not listening at all to me. The funny part of all of this (and there is a funny part to this) is that **God was listening all along**. I come to realize that **I wasn't listening to Him**.

It was a Sunday afternoon where I was passing a church. I was not sure what time of day it was. I couldn't tell the time as far as minutes, hours or seconds that passed. All I knew was while people were coming out of the church, a brother was coming out and saw me passing the church. I must have really been looking bad, or really malnourished because he stopped me and asked me my name. As I told him my name, he seemed to have had a sense of my struggles. At that time, it was as if he knew something about me. He prophesied to me and told me that I did not belong out here in these streets. It was as if he knew as I was struggling and needed the help. He told me who he was and he offered me something to eat. We went out to eat and we talked for a couple of hours. Without hesitation, he offered me a room in his house to stay until I was able to get on my feet. I did not know this brother. I didn't know what his motive were. At this point in time, I didn't care. All I knew was that someone cared enough to take me in. I was smelling bad. I was hungry. I was alone. I needed help. Once I got there, I finally realized why he took me in. He took me in because of his own personal story. I was hesitant at first because I wasn't sure of his motives. When we sat down to talk, he told me that he used to be homeless also. Someone took him in, fed and clothed him and in return, he did the same. I started crying and laughing at the same time because I was so grateful and appreciative for his kindness and generosity. All he asked of me was when I'd get back on my feet and able to reach my goals again, it was the hope that I would pass this same kindness on to someone else who would need it.

Another thing I didn't know at the time was that **God was shaping and molding me all along,** teaching me on this journey that **success was not about the riches of the world, but the riches of your heart and what you can do to serve Him and others.**

When I was a child growing up, we were always taught Hebrews 13:5.

> **Hebrews 13:5 – Keep your lives free from the love of money and be content with what you have because God has said, "Never will I leave you; never will I forsake you."**

I never forgot this verse as a child. However, I must have put it away somewhere in my sub-conscious and forgot the meaning of this passage. Everywhere I go (now), I carry it with me in my heart and soul. This is my true success in life today. I just didn't think about it back then and how this verse would shape me into learning about what true success really was. I also never forgot the kindness of this stranger. I never forgot what this stranger requested of me to do once I'd got back on my feet. I'd believe that he would be proud of me. To God be the glory.

As you can see now from reading this book, that I have come a long way from this journey and have found true *success.* I have come to learn that *success* is being thankful and grateful for this moment (and every moment) in time that we are living in the now (the present). Success is knowing that the wealth of the world means nothing because all of this can be taken away in a split second … in the blinking of an eye. I have learned that my past experience was only preparation for my true understanding of what was about to become the true meaning of *success* for my life. What I am giving to the world as far as what knowledge I have gained, I am passing this knowledge on. I have true success in being thankful for what I have and cherishing the present. I am not rich in material wealth. However, I am rich in knowledge, and the spirit to be of help to others. *Success for me is now measured by my worth and meaning in life.* In my journey towards becoming a doctor, I had to become a human being all over again. I had to trust in someone other than myself. Trusting in myself was not working. *I had to trust fully in God and not my own understanding.* I had to go through my own personal journey and ask myself questions such as:

1. Now that I know what success is, what should now be my matter of concern?
2. Now that success is not about wealth, what should my priority be?
3. Now that success no longer concerns the wealth of the world, what will be my true measure of success?

I have come to learn that the true measure of *success* is passing on what I have learned and making sure that I do it with compassion, love, empowerment, and with the love of God supporting me all the way. I know that my lesson on *success* did not just happen by accident. It was planned by God for me to pass this way. My purpose from here on end was to empower others and realize that this gift that was given to me was not mine alone … but through lessons learned it was to be passed on so that others will not necessarily have to struggle as I did.

Do you find yourself struggling with *success*? Do you ever wonder if you value success more than your own self -worth? Let's see if you are on the right track. Take a moment to answer a total of six (6) short questions. Try to be as honest and true to yourself as possible.

1. Are you a goal setter or a wishful thinker?

    _____

2. Have you set a goal for yourself within the past month? _____
3. Did you meet that goal? _____
4. If you met that goal, did you feel success? _____
5. Describe in a few words what success felt like:

    _____

    _____

    _____

    _____

    _____

6. If you didn't meet that goal you set for yourself, what stopped you from meeting that goal?

    _____

    _____

    _____

    _____

I know at this point, there are some things that you are thinking about and nodding your head in disbelief because you probably can identify with most of your failures instead of your successes. Did it take you longer to think of a goal that you completed with success? Did it take you a while to even think of a goal that you set for yourself and succeeded completely?

I would like for you to now consider some of the reasons why we get stuck on the word, "success." I hold many life coaching sessions and many seminars on how to be the best "YOU" and discovering your success through loving and embracing your self- worth. In these sessions I've conducted, many of those who struggled with the word and idea of *success*. Most of those seeking a better life, measured *success* by their revenue and finances, their influence they were making on their family, friends and peers and by the things that they have completed (and not completed) in their journey to what they thought was *success* by material growth. What I would like for you to start considering now is that many of us have our own ideas and definitions about *success*. Your ideas and thoughts about success seems to be focused around your accomplishments and measuring your life by your work, what you have done so far and how much you have gained (instead of accomplished).

Here are four more questions that I would like for you to complete to see how you measure success. Remember to answer as honestly and truthfully as possible. It's all about you.

7. Do you see success as immediate or a process?

   _____

   _____

8. Do you consider yourself successful?

   _____

   _____

9. If you consider yourself successful, name some of the ways you've reached that point.

   _____

   _____

   _____

   _____

10. If you do not consider yourself successful, what is holding you back from considering yourself successful?

    _____

    _____

    _____

    _____

If you have completed this section with all honesty and truth, you will find that success had nothing to do with finances, influences, status or material growth. Now, don't misunderstand what I am saying. Finances, influences or status can be considered as a result of the success. However, that is not *success* for you. Let me repeat that statement for you ..." Finances, influences or status can be considered as a result of the success ... that is not success for you."

Everyone desires and wants success. However, success is not having the best job in the world. Success is not even having the best marriage, plenty of vacations, or maybe that Porsche you may have parked in your garage. **Success is not based on prosperity.** Any success that we have comes from several factors that we need to examine and practice.

Success is measured by Character:

If any of you should die today, you would never been known for what you have really done or accomplished in life. Of course, what you have done will be printed in the obituary. However, that will not matter when someone stands on the pulpit to talk about your life. You will probably be highlighted for your *character.* Our character tells a lot about us, who we were, and who we are. Our character will determine our success.

If you find yourself, anxious, bewildered, bored, cautious, cold-hearted, conceited, dangerous, dishonest, doubtful, frustrated, greedy, impatient and impulsive, you will find yourself with much unhappiness, pain and the direction to self-doubt, leading to failure in reaching your success. These are characteristics that are real that sometimes possess, and take over our lives at times because we seek the wrong type of success. These negative characteristics will take over and then take the form of material worth. You will become consumed with wanting the earthly, material gains of the world instead of those qualities needed to discover your full potential for excellence. If you seek for the material successes, you will never achieve the true goal of happiness and success that we so seek.

The true qualities of success are the ones who finds their true talents in how to develop ways to help themselves and others, develop a sense of pride in working hard and achieving goals that will make a difference in not only your life, but in the lives of others while maintaining the characteristics of being attentive, compassionate, confident, cooperative, dependable, enthusiastic, exciting, helpful and hopeful.

Success surely proved to become one of the most deadly words for me. I saw how it prevented me from being the best that I could be … yet showed me how to use it to enhance my life by thinking of someone other than myself and making sure that character plays a big part in being the best you can be. When all is said and done at the end of your life … how will you want people to remember your success … by your wealth … or by your character?

Do not be anxious about anything, but in everything
by prayer and supplication with thanksgiving let
your requests be made known to God.
Phillipians 4:6

From the rising of the sun...til the going down of the same, I
pray when I am thankful for the blessings, when I am down
in despair and can't lift up my head enough to see the sun
shining, and when I need to pray for others as well as myself.
Well, I guess that would mean "praying without ceasing"...
all day, everyday. Prayer changes things...especially our lives.
Dr. Thomas L. Page

"PRAYER"

Now who would have thought that PRAYER would have been one of the deadliest words that I selected that would keep us from becoming the best we can be. Everything that I do in my life starts out with a prayer. Before writing this book, I prayed. Every morning before I put my feet on the floor I pray. Before I go to bed at night I pray. Before I eat my meals or before I make any major decisions that affects my life, I pray. So, I guess you are wondering that if I am doing all of this praying, why would I consider *prayer* one of the deadliest words. Before I explain the full detail on why, let's start with the idea of prayer, and what prayer should be.

Many theologians and those in the ministry who preach and write about prayer would say that prayer is a direct line to Heaven.

Prayer is a communication process that gives us permission to talk with God. It has been written that prayer presupposes a belief in the personality of God, his ability and willingness to communicate with us, his personal control of all things, and of all his creatures and all their actions.

So now to get to the heart of the matter, it would be assumed that in order for a person to pray, one must believe in something greater than themselves. For someone such as myself, I would believe in the Lord God Almighty ... Jesus Christ ... My Savior ... make of Heaven and Earth.

There are many scriptures in the Bible that talks about prayer and the supplication of prayer, where it would be known that if one prays, God would hear their prayers and they would be answered. For example:

> 2 Chronicles 7:14: "If my people, which are called by my name, shall humble themselves, and pray, and seek my face, and turn from their wicked ways; then will I hear from Heaven, and will forgive their sin, and will heal their land."

> Isaiah 55:6: "Seek ye the Lord while He may be found, call ye upon Him while He is near."

> Job 8:5: "If you would seek God early, and make your supplications to the Almighty;"

I only referenced a few scriptures just to make a point of what prayer is and how prayer may be verbal, mental constant, formal ... and one of the deadliest words we use.

Let me be one who can testify and confirm that prayer works. Throughout my whole life, prayer has been the one constant thing, that guiding force in my life that has kept me grounded, focused, safe, and assured. Whenever my life was in total chaos, prayer kept me in a place of calm. When people in my life whom I loved the most and cherished passed away, it was prayer that linked me to the hope of seeing them again. Prayer made me realize that in talking to someone much greater than myself, I would receive the comfort in knowing that my prayers would not just be answered ... but my prayers would be heard, being accepted as sincere from me. It is through prayer that I became a humbled person, knowing that I was insignificant and unworthy of His grace because of my sins. Because of my sins, prayer helped me to realize that it was not through my will that I am being heard, comforted, and forgiven, but through HIS will that all things were done in accordance to Him. So prayer works.

Here is where prayer can be a deadly word to many who really wants to change their lives but find it so hard (and a struggle) to make a better life for themselves through prayer.

There are those who don't *believe* in prayer:

In my last book, *"When Love Is Not Enough: Bringing Spirituality and Coping Back to Families and Homes (2011),* I wrote to parents: "All sons ... no matter what age wants to hear that He is loved, valued and special. To bring him to the next level ... which is prayer, just say to him, **"I have been praying for you and your safety, can I pray with you?"** He may say no at first, but don't give up. Keep asking on a daily basis. Once you start praying and getting into the practice of talking to God every day, your son will see the difference in you and your behavior in how you treat him now and will start becoming more involved in the family and may begin praying with you. So, I will say this to you like God has told us many times ... "I will never leave you nor forsake you." Use these words to remember not to give up on your adolescent or young adult males. Do not leave them nor forsake them. Be ever present. Be that parent that they need you to be ... and I can assure you the best results. *For when love is not enough ... there is spirituality and unification in the family."*

When I went on tour for my first book, I had several sessions with families and found that there were parents who didn't pray with their young men (or daughters) because they didn't believe in prayer themselves. They didn't (and wouldn't) believe in a God that would make them suffer as they were suffering in their homes and communities. This reality that some people did not believe in the power of prayer changed the lives of young people everywhere, causing a reaction of mistrust and anger that would give them nothing to hope for or believe in. There were many times I would leave a center heartbroken, but not defeated. I've come to realize that through my prayers, even the adults that didn't believe in prayer came to an understanding. They had come to believe that prayer was not an immediate answer for God to take care of problems immediately and when they needed something right away. Prayer had to be offered in faith, knowing that when we prayed, we may never see God's work visibly, but **trust** that He was (and is) the hearer and answer of our prayers, and will deliver our answers at the time we will need it the most. This comes to the next struggle:

There are those who don't *trust* in prayer:

I have friends in my life today that still don't trust in prayer. I have to admit, their lives are a mess, but won't trust in what prayer can do. So, they leave it to me or someone else in the church to pray for them. I have to laugh sometimes because no matter how much I pray for them, one must pray for themselves as well to receive the blessing that is being requested.

I have to make a confession here. When growing up and before I gave myself fully to Christ, I didn't trust prayer, either. I would fake a good game because everyone else was doing it. It was something to do when I only got in trouble ... and when I got in trouble, I would become sarcastic and usually say, "This is why I don't trust prayer." Even after giving myself to Christ, I finally realized how prayer really worked and the challenge of trusting prayer. On December 7, 2000, not only was my faith tested, but my prayer life was tested.

I prayed for a miracle to help my father recover from congestive heart failure. I knew that being a child of God that all I had to do was pray and God would answer the desires of my heart. Well, prayer (or what I thought was prayer) didn't work. My father died. This feeling of helplessness left me with false hopes in a God who promised me that if I would pray, my prayers would be answered. I thought that as someone who came to Christ, I was forgiven for my sins and I would be covered under the banner of his love. I also thought that meant my family (when I prayed for them) would always be protected. **I always thought my will was enough.** However, there was a lesson I missed somewhere in my early years of being saved ... something I learned from not only my father's death, but the death of my mother also in June of 2009. I learned that my prayers did work. However, the prayer I asked for was not the prayer of my will. **I'd learned that day that it was never "my will." It was "God's will" that needed to be done.** It wasn't until my father's funeral when we did the *"Lord's Prayer"* where I finally knew how to trust in prayer. There is a passage where it stated, "Our Father, who art in Heaven, hallowed be thy name. Thy Kingdom come, **thy will be done**, on earth as it is in Heaven. It threw me for a loop because there were many times when I really didn't trust in prayer to work. I had to realize that prayer wasn't about my will, but the will of the Heavenly Father to do what was best for those who were suffering on Earth.

As a firm believer of prayer, I think about those who are not sure if they can trust prayer. Have you ever been one who wasn't sure if you trusted prayer? What were your circumstances? To help you through the process of knowing if you trust in prayer, name a time where you prayed to God for something and you felt that He did not answer your prayer: _____

_____

_____

_____

_____

How did you pray? _____

_____

_____

_____

_____

Was it for your sake (will)? Yes_____ No_____

If you answered yes, for your sake, you are not alone in your answer. We have to trust that the prayers we render to God is not for our will ... but for His (God's) will ... that His will be done. **We are not God**. Our will does not have the power to heal. Our will only bring the communication to the One who has the will to make things happen. Also know, that trusting in prayer is about knowing who is in control. We are not in control. That is why prayer is so crucial in our spiritual lives. Even though God is in control, within the context of that control, He has given us liberties to act upon it, by projecting our will to Him.

The only way you know that you can trust prayer, is by holding on and believing His will through the roughest times in your life, by understanding who can determine the best and the worst of something in your life, and allowing Him to be the One who has all of the facts at their disposal to do what is right for you when you need an answer. If we had that capability ourselves, we wouldn't need prayer. You should now be able to recognize that even as a person who is fully content in their lives, I still struggle and live in a world where I am being rejected, hurt and subjected to pain. Jesus was done the same way. So why would I think that would exempt me from trials and tribulations if He had to be exposed to the suffering He went through?

There is also something that I would like for you to reflect on. God's will gives us the opportunities we need to develop and grow from whatever will He has decided for our lives. It doesn't mean that we have to like the outcomes (like death of loved ones, etc.) or turn away because it hurts too much for the moment. It only means that we need to give ourselves a break, and take the time and opportunity to mature through the difficult times and dimensions of God's divine will.

There are those who don't *respect* prayer:

Before I get into this section, I would like for you to respond to just a few questions that would probably give you a little insight of people who do not respect prayer.

1. Do you know someone in your life who has ever said to you, "Don't pray for me ... pray for yourself? _____
2. Have you had someone in your life that was envious of you for your prayer life? _____
3. Is that person someone you trust? _____
4. Do you still maintain communication with people who do not consider prayer as an important part of their life? _____
5. Do you live with someone who does not respect your prayer life? _____

If you have answered "yes" to any of these questions, you can believe that you possibly have a non-believer amongst your midst, or someone who does not respect prayer. I have learned through my journey and through many life coaching sessions, learning from the many experiences of those who changed their lives for the better, are going to be people who will not respect you for what you believe. We all have various times that require dealing with negative people. However, if you are truly attempting at making your life better, and want to experience the best that life has to offer you, it will be necessary to separate yourself from that person, especially if this person has an effect on you. It is not your responsibility to show them their faults. It is not our place to argue the point of prayer. Here are some suggested points that I would like to suggest as a way of making sure your prayer life stays intact and not interrupted by those who cannot respect prayer:

1. Remain humble

Try not to judge the person in your life who does not respect prayer. You can see them as a creation of God who has a sinful habit that needs to be dealt with by God (and not you). He/She is still a child and a creation by God that still needs your respect, your attention and love. In Galatians 6:1, we are reminded of the following: "Brothers and sisters, if someone is caught in a sin, you who live by the spirit should restore that person gently. But watch yourselves, or you also may be tempted'. This leads me to my next point.

2. Pray for wisdom.

The purpose here is not to pray for the person who is just not respecting prayer. However, you are praying for yourself. You are praying that God gives you wisdom to reveal a clear plan of action for you, especially if it someone you live with or deal with in your everyday life. Ask God to give you the wisdom to show favor, tactfulness and an approach that will demonstrate strength as a believer, without violating this person's dignity, no matter how aggravating and obnoxious they become. And if none of these approaches work.

3. Limit your contact so that your life will be enhanced.

And whenever you stand praying, forgive, if you have anything against anyone, so that your Father also who is in heaven may forgive you your trespasses.

Mark 11:25

I have experienced hurt to the depths that would lead me to hate. However, I have a God who has forgiven me for things I may have done much worse than others may have done to me. The best thing that I could ever do to honor God and His word is to "forgive".

Dr. Thomas L Page

"FORGIVE"

Of the seven deadliest words that holds us back, *forgive* is the one word that has been the hardest hurdle for me to get over. This word has changed the directions in my life so many times due to the fact that there has been so many people and circumstances that has caused me to forgive and/or seek forgiveness. *Forgiveness* is not just something we take on and take off like a coat and hat. Forgiveness is the act of forgiving. Forgiveness is no longer carrying resentment or harboring ill feelings towards a person that has hurt you in the past. *Forgiveness* is being able to let go of whatever hurt and anger you are holding against someone and resolving the situation not only with that person, but within your heart. It took me a long time to learn this. I am not ashamed nor embarrassed to say that it took me up until my late 40's to learn the true meaning of forgiveness.

Why do we forgive? Throughout our lives, we set ourselves in a place where if we don't forgive, we can become bitter, cold, heartless people. We carry this bitterness and hatred inside of us without ever really knowing why and start developing a mental state of silence, a shell within ourselves … shutting ourselves from the joy and happiness that we have been so freely given in life. Someone could say one comment that could hurt you and set you back. The comments or harsh words that are said to you can do something to you that makes you believe in your heart that you are not worthy of that person's love and respect. So, instead of just dealing with the situation or hurt head on, we go within ourselves and stop communicating. Sometimes we not only stop communicating with that person, but we close up and shut ourselves out from the people who love us the most. We block the faith we have built as a child for resilience because that hurt is so deep from that person who has hurt us that we go back to that place where we were once safe and don't want to come back out of that safety net. Most of all, we turn our backs from the God who gives us a reason for waking up in the morning, finding several reasons to give thanks and seeking and mapping out our purpose in life. We get mad at our Supreme Being for letting this happen to us. We get mad at ourselves for getting into this position of helplessness and not knowing how to let go of this hurt and anger. So now, your whole mental state is effecting your physical state. This hurt has you so bound up in grief that you start to believe that you are getting physically ill, falling into a deep depression that makes you want to roll up in a ball and just give up on everything you worked so hard for in life.

Yes, I know that feeling all too well. I can remember where I felt all of these feelings throughout my life and how far back it took me to realize that if I didn't forgive or have forgiveness in my heart, I would be stuck for life on a road going nowhere. I can think back on two of the most dangerous times in my life where *forgiveness* was a deadly word for me. I remember how the death of my mother caused me to challenge myself in forgiving members of my immediate family. The biggest challenge of all was in forgiving myself for letting her die. I thought I did everything right to keep her alive and keep her on earth for as long as I could. I would visit Momma every day in the hospital. I would make sure that she was given the best of care and I would sit with her every night and watch her sleep until I knew it was alright for me to leave for the night. I knew all of the doctors and nurses by name and kept a daily log on the things I needed to do to make sure that Momma was taken care of. The day of her death, all I could remember was that while putting her in the bed for the last time, my mother had a look that was unknown to me, as if she was telling me to prepare myself. Little did I know that it was that look of content and readiness to die that I had to prepare for. She looked at me and told me that she was tired and she wanted to be alone. In my whole life, my mother never wanted to be alone. I told her that I would be right here and I'm not going anywhere. It was then she told me, "I am ready to take my rest". With that, I knew what that look meant for me. I told Momma that I loved her and kissed her ever so gently on the forehead, and I told her that it is alright to go to sleep. I told her to go to sleep and everything will be ok. A few hours later, the woman I knew as my "Momma" was gone. All I could think of was how could I forgive myself for letting her die and how could this have happened when I did everything in my power to keep her with us.

Part of *forgiveness* was knowing that I didn't have control of this situation, and I had to come to the reality that Momma wasn't going to live forever. There was going to be a time when I had to face the fact that she raised me to know how to love and never give up on your dreams. She taught me how to become independent and taught me how to trust in somebody bigger than her and myself. Along with that, she always taught our family how to forgive, even though that lesson took me a while to learn.

Two nights before she died, we talked about forgiveness and how she wanted me to forgive my son for walking out of my life and not giving me any reason as to why he walked out on the one who loved and cared for him the most. Even though the reason became clear later on in life, she wanted me to forgive myself for taking the blame all on myself and not just letting my son "go through his own valley". This term meant going through his own struggles and working through them. She knew what he was going through and she always told me that he was going to come back, talk to me and to just give him time. She kept telling me throughout that night that he loved me and he is going to come back to reconcile with me. No matter how old we (my brothers and sisters) were, Momma could still read all of our faces and knew when something was bothering us. She helped me to realize forgiveness when we talked about all of the hurt she went through in her life and how she had to come to grips with forgiving others as well as herself. She regretted how she deprived us of meeting all of her brothers and sisters and not giving us the opportunity in getting to know them. She had 21 brothers and sisters (not including herself). We only got to meet one sister … Aunt Josie Mae. She regretted how she was hurt that we (my son and I) never got the chance to reconcile while she was still here. She wanted to see that so badly. She wanted to see her great grandchild once more. However she told me he stopped coming by and how he never let her see her great grandchild again. She thought that she did something wrong. However, she said, without hesitation, "Love the sinner … not the sin … if I can forgive my own grandson, you can surely forgive your son." That put everything in perspective for me. That put the word "forgive" into a whole different level of understanding that I never had before.

That is when the word *forgive* became real for me. Mom and I talked for hours about forgiveness. I never knew how much my mother was carrying my burden and hurt until that night. It made me realize that if she can forgive my son for hurting me and her, who was I to hold grudges. It was all about *forgiveness* for her. It was all about *forgiveness* in order for me to move forward and make the change in my life for the better.

In the same way, I remember all too well the death of my father and how I had the hardest time in thinking of how I was going to forgive him for dying on me at the time when I thought I needed him the most. I knew that death did not have a time limit. I knew that death came unexpectedly. However, I thought that the God I knew, knew the thoughts of my heart and how I needed "Pop" to be alive for my mother and for me. I really didn't care about the rest of the family at the time. All I knew was that I needed him in my life. I always thought that my father would be here for me. I could not see life without my "Pop". When he died, *forgiveness* was not an option for me. My thoughts were all over the place and all I could think of at the time was, "What did I do wrong"?

I kept playing back in my head one day before he died the conversation I had with him at the hospital. I knew that "Pop" wasn't really himself. He seemed really quiet and did not have much to say. He kept staring at the wall and then his eyes went back on me as to see if I was still sitting there. For some reason or another, I would always have a conversation for him. That night, I just kept staring at him as if it was my last time seeing him alive. Little did I know that it would be my very last stare of him alive. I got up out of the chair and went to the bed. I asked him if he was alright. He told me that he was worried about Christine and he made me promise to take care of her if something happened to him. I told him that he wasn't going anywhere and that God didn't want him yet. He didn't find that very funny and he told me to make a promise to him that if anything happened to him, I would take care of Christine. He was very adamant about it. I made the promise and told him that I would take care of her if anything happened to him. Immediately after that, he said, "I'm ready to go home". I told him that he was going to go home tomorrow, so you don't have to worry about that. Then he looked at me with tears in his eyes and said, "I'm ready to go home, Baby". It was as if my life was cut short. I knew what he meant, and I had to let him know that I understood. I tried fighting back the tears to not let him show my fear and worry. However, I could not hold back tears. All I did was rubbed his forehead, kissed it, and told him that everything was going to be ok. I'll take care of things for him. The next day he went home. I got a call from the house that "Pop" was rushed to the hospital and he was not responding. On the way to the hospital, it's as if a warm gentle breeze blew on my neck while driving to my parent's house. I knew that must have been a sign from my "Pop" that all was finished on his part and now I had to take over. As I got to the hospital, they had pronounce him dead. I went into the room where he was and I just sat next to him while they were cleaning him up. As they took off his wedding band to give to me, all I could think about was how selfish he was to leave me here alone with Christine (Momma) to take care of her. That was his responsibility. I could not forgive him for doing this to me. I could not forgive myself for letting him die. I thought I had done everything right to keep him alive. I'd always taken him to the VA Hospital as I became old enough to drive. That was my responsibility. I was there when they had to take him to the hospital to get his leg amputated, made sure that he had the support that he needed and he wasn't left alone. I was there. That was my responsibility. I did everything a son could do to make sure that he would live a long life. As like Christine, part of understanding the concept of the word "forgive" was knowing that I didn't have control of this situation, and I had to come to the reality that "Pop" wasn't going to live forever. It wasn't until the last second in the room where my father died with his eyes opened and I saw a smile. I saw the peace on his face that told me that everything is right with him now. I had to make it right with myself. I had to make it right with my Heavenly Father. Once I took my hand to close his eyes, I blamed myself and I blamed God for taking him away from me, even though He knew that I did all I could possibly do as a son and a human being. When I saw that smile on his face, I knew he (along with the Heavenly Father) was looking down on me and they both had forgiven me for my thoughts. I had to forgive myself for being so hard on myself, and I had to ask God for his forgiveness and to change my heart. I came to the realization that we have no control over peoples' lives, but we do have control over how to forgive.

I have come to learn that there is a true art of learning how to forgive. It starts with yourself. Knowing that you don't have control over anyone's life but your own should help you to realize that 1) You can overcome any obstacle just by learning to "let go ... and let God" and 2) The sooner you learn that and stop fighting God at every corner trying to take revenge for yourself, the more you will understand that you can forgive just as easily as harboring deep, hurt feelings, taking the moment to realize what is the real issue behind your anger and learning how to channel that anger into something great. If you cannot learn to forgive, you should read this chapter over again.

But by the grace of God I am what I am, and His grace toward me did not prove vain; but I labored even more than all of them, yet not I, but the grace of God with me.
I Corinthians 15:10

"But"...The only word small enough to get us into big trouble. "But"...Big enough to keep us from being negative and small minded."
Dr. Thomas L. Page

"BUT ..."

In developing this book, I was thinking of putting the two words "but" and "if" together. Once I started organizing my thoughts and diagramming everything when it came to these two words, it was clear to me that these two words ... as deadly as they are ... had to be separated.

Many of us are all too familiar with the word "but." Some people carry the biggest "Buts" in the world. Do you know of anyone who carries a big "but"? Do they seem to carry their "but" with them every place they go? Could you be carrying a big "but" of your own? How do you know when you are carrying too much "but"?

Well, this is one of the chapters that I have researched and been waiting to write. This word holds a special place in my heart because I can truly say that this is one of the deadliest words that I have experienced with many in my life coaching sessions and especially dealing with loved ones. I have some loved ones who I see with such great potential, and has every tool they need to be the best they can be. However, they made it a choice to just sit and be docile. Every excuse seems to be made under the sun why things do not get done in their lives. I have done everything I could except take them by the hand to guide them through the process. So, now I have learned to back away and let them deal with their own "buts."

So as a lifeline to help those who are stuck with "buts" in their lives, take a few minutes to complete the seven statements below. Answer the questions as if it is pertaining to your life. I have selected these particular questions because many can identify with them and have gone through many of these statements before. Try to be as honest and truthful as you can.

1. I would love to _____,
   but I am so busy.
2. I will sign up to _____,
   but I need to get more information first.
3. I would love to _____
   but I don't have time for that.
4. I would love to get _____
   for myself, ***but*** I can't afford it.
5. _____
   might work for some people, ***but*** not for me.
6. I would love to _____
   but it's not the right time.
7. I would say to talk about _____
   but no one really cares what I think.

While you were completing this exercise, did you have a déjà vu at some point? Did any of these statements look familiar to you? Of course they have. How many times have you wanted something while you were window shopping and you said, "I would get that, but I can't afford it."? How many times have we wanted to go on a vacation and before we can complete our thoughts fully, you stop in the middle of your conversation and said, "But I don't have the money" or "but it's not the right time."? Even in your lives today, there are so many things that many of you would like to do, say, and act upon. However, you are still stuck with your "but."

I chose "but" as one of the deadliest words because of the effect that it has on our lives. This 3 letter word has such an effect on us, it literally controls us without you even realizing it. Let me give you some examples that will hit home for some of you. Check off any of the list that applies to you. Even if you have thought about it, but have not yet saw through the activity ... check it off.

A FEW OF THE "BUTS" THAT HOLD US BACK FROM BEING THE BEST YOU CAN BE"

_____ "I would complete my education, BUT ..."

_____ "I would go to the gym to get in shape, BUT ..."

_____ "I would go back to church, BUT ..."

_____ "I knew I was wrong and I should apologize, BUT ..."

_____ "I know that I could do that job, BUT ..."

_____ "I would love do that one day, BUT ..."

_____ "I should go on a date, BUT ..."

This was not an exercise to call you out or blame you for letting a small word such as "but" get in the way of being the best you can be. As I said before, some of you may not even realize that you are doing it, or you have said it so many times in your journey that it has become a habit for you. It is really amazing how many peoples' lives have been altered just by interjecting the word "but" into it. "But" stops you from accomplishing the very thing you want to do the most.

When we interject the word "but" in our daily conversations, we are just making excuses for the things that are scaring us, bringing us fear, or anticipating failure (without even attempting the activity first). As soon as you incorporate the word "BUT" into your vocabulary, you start losing control to accomplish what you want out of life. You are literally surrendering to whatever your excuse is. Your excuse can be that of dating, losing weight, age, disability, or even just plain laziness.

I had a whole lot of **"BUTS"** through my journey here. I am definitely not the exception to the rule. I learned a valuable lesson on how just the word **"BUT,"** can alter and change your life. All of my life, I wanted to work in the mental health field in the area of life coaching. I wanted to make a difference in the lives of those who were hurting and really wanted to help them make the best out of their lives. I was young, just starting college and didn't know how to handle the freedom that I was given. I was given a scholarship. However, did not maintain it because my GPA ended up to be 1.6. Here, I lost the scholarship and owed money to the college. So, my **BUT** was that I could not finish school because I had messed up in school and I couldn't get my transcripts until I had paid the bill. With no job, I was stuck.

God blessed me with a second chance. I took it and received my Bachelors. However, the bachelors that I received was not in the field I needed to get into the mental health field. So now, my new **BUT** was that I will go back to get the right degree to get into life coaching, BUT I had to go to work to get some money first. It took over 14 years to get past the many more **BUTS** before reaching my goal.

The difference here is that I never gave up the dream. I never gave up the vision. I chipped away each layer of excuses until one day, I finally said, "Enough is enough!" I was tired of making excuses. IT WAS MY CHOICE:

- To mess up the scholarship I was given

- To have sex
- To have children
- To procrastinate
- To settle for a low paying job
- To wait for something better to come instead of going for it.
- To wait until I got older to do something about it.

Know that the list I made is mine. These are not anyone else's excuses. These for me were the results of letting **BUT** get in the way of being the best I can be.

Mind you, I have "to have children" on the list. God has blessed me with sons that I love and cherish with all of my heart, and a beautiful niece whom I raised with my mom & pop when my sister passed. My sons and daughter were God's gift to me. Because of them, I stopped using *"BUT"* as an excuse, got my butt in gear and did something about it. By changing my thought process and given something to get up for in the morning (with my eyes on the prize), to enhance and work for (as far as a new goal and vision), the *"BUT"* in my life now became "ACTION," and the rest is history.

Yes, the word **BUT** is a deadly word. However, the only time the word "**BUT**" should be referenced is only in the Bible. That is the only time I use it because of the positive, rich and amazing hope it brings for us as a people ... "BUT GOD":

Ephesians 2:4-5 - **But God**, being rich in mercy, because of the great love with which he loved us, even when we were dead in our trespasses, made us alive together with Christ— by grace you have been saved ..."

Romans 5:8 - **but God** shows his love for us in that while we were still sinners, Christ died for us.

Psalm 86:15 - But you, O Lord, are a God merciful and gracious, slow to anger and abounding in steadfast love and faithfulness.

Knowing that we are not God, we, here on earth, still struggling with our "*BUT.*" Before I start suggesting solutions, I would like to give you a few more facts to understand and help you see where you might be in your journey if you are struggling with your "*BUT.*" If you have gotten to this point of the book, it is safe to say that you have received some great information already and should be steps closer to preparing for a positive change in your life.

At this point, it is important to understand that the word "*BUT,*" could truly mess with your self-esteem. Some of you who are reading this may already have that feeling. If you are not sure of the signs, let me attempt to explain it to you.

If you find yourself in a place of uncertainty, and you are questioning and doubting yourself, and holding on to the feelings, words, and actions of other people instead of your own, this is a real sign that you are dealing with an issue of self-esteem. When you use the word *BUT* to make excuses for why your life is not where you want it to be, you start doubting yourself and this in turn, start you to value your self-worth as being "shallow" or "worthless."

When you get to this point, you begin to shut yourself down by avoiding people and conflicts. You demonstrate this in a number of ways, through the following actions:

- Avoiding those who remind you of what you are missing in your life.
- Avoiding those who remind you of the *BUT* in your life that is still active.
- Pretending that everything is alright when it is definitely not.

- Lying to others and yourself to cover up the real truth that things are not working out as you had planned
- You become defensive over everything. Instead of seeing the concern that others may be having for you, it is seen as a personal attack.

As this process continually unfolds, you may probably come to the realization that over time, you have already convinced yourself that you will not be able to achieve that goal and vision you once had for yourself. You will then stop caring about whether or not you achieved that goal or anything else that was of hope for you.

I hope that I have painted a clear picture of how your *"BUT"* could end up if you are not careful and start taking action now. I will begin to open some positive doors for you in order that you may find a pinhole of light to getting started on your new journey to a better life that you want to have.

Light at the End of a Dark Tunnel ...

It is now time for you to start changing your *"BUT"* into something better. I would like to give you some suggestions to help you start the process of getting back on your feet and heading forward to the goal you intended to make from day one. It is never too late. I am a living witness as to what God can do, no matter what age.

The first thing that I would like for you to do is to get your pencil/pen ready and begin to start your process. Once you follow this process, I believe that this can be a start for you as it has been for those whom I have life coached.

STEP ONE:

Now that you have your pencil/pen in hand, I would like for you to write down this AFFIRMATION as a constant reminder every time you feel yourself as less than what you should be in your journey. You are making a promise to yourself and you are writing this to the most important person in your circle ... YOU. You are the one that matters at this point and you have to now be dedicated to yourself:

AFFIRMATION:

I AM NOW IN CHARGE OF MY OWN LIFE AND WILL NOT MAKE ANY TYPE OF EXCUSES FROM REACHING MY GOAL. MY GOAL IS MORE IMPORTANT THAN MY EXCUSES. I AM CAPABLE OF DOING EXTRAORDINARY THINGS AND IT IS UP TO ME TO TAKE THE TIME AND MAKE THE EFFORT TO COMPLETE MY GOAL.

_____

_____

_____

_____

_____

_____

_____

_____

_____

_____

Signature Date

STEP TWO:

Create **ONE** goal that you would like to make for yourself at this point in time. Make it a goal that is **REACHABLE**. The biggest victories always start out with a small goal and grows from there.

A PERSONAL GOAL THAT I WOULD LIKE TO MAKE FOR MYSELF IS:

_____

_____

_____

_____

_____

_____

STEP THREE:

Create a *PLAN A.*

Now that you have your Affirmation complete, your goal is in place, now what will your plan to enforce that goal look like? Where do you begin the process? Let's start here:

WHO: Write your name so that you will validate yourself.

_____

_____

WHAT: (What is the exact plan you want to do in order to meet your personal goal?

Example: Goal: I want to run for a city office position.

WHAT: I will complete the application in order to qualify.

_____

_____

WHEN:

- Pick a day that you will be carrying out this particular task.
- Make sure that you confirm a time for yourself so that you will prepare.

_____

_____

_____

WHERE:

- Know the exact place on where you need to go.
- Know how you are going to get there ... plan ahead.
- Have an alternate way to get there just in case your first plan falls through.

WHY:

Specify and write down in detail why you are doing it this way. Do not rewrite "because this is my goal." Write down why you are going about it the way you are to make sure that you are clear of everything you are doing.

_____

_____

_____

HOW: Measuring your progress

In this section, the HOW is the outcome that should result in getting your goal completed. This part should only be answered after you have completed the goal. This should include:

- Whether you have (or have not completed) your goal?
- If you have completed your goal, this is the time where you write your successes on how you made it work for you.

_____

_____

_____

_____

Celebrate your victory. Start on your next goal that you would like to achieve.

- If you did not complete your goal, go through your steps and write down where you believe it didn't work for you.

_____

_____

_____

_____

Celebrate the fact that you followed through on your goal. This will be a victory in itself. Once you have enjoyed your moment, create a PLAN B. Even though Plan A did not work the way you had intended, you develop another plan to make sure you get it done. Plan B should always include some type of support from someone who can assist and be a support for you. This will ensure that you will succeed by not giving up.

"...if my people, who are called by my name, will humble themselves and pray and seek my face and turn from their wicked ways, then I will hear from heaven, and I will forgive their sin and will heal their land."
2 Chronicles 7:14

"IF ..."

I wasn't quite sure how to introduce the next deadliest word that sometimes prevents us from moving forward. However, it is one of the smallest words next to the word "A," but seems to have the biggest impact in our lives. I would like to think that it would have been easy to introduce this word in just a blanket statement. Instead, I am going to introduce this word in the form of a sentence.

"If you were to die tomorrow, what would be the biggest "IF" you would regret the most?

All of our lives seems to center around two of the smallest words with the biggest impact ... "IF" and "BUT."

How many times in our lives have we made statements using the word "if" and thinking "If only" or "What if." In my journey through life, I have come to realize that the only thing that was holding me back from getting the things I wanted done the most was myself and my "If's." It's really hard to imagine how much time I have wasted with the word "If," procrastinating, putting off when I know that I could have accomplished many more things that could have made my life much easier and better for me.

Now, I take nothing for granted. I am blessed and thankful for my life and all that I have accomplished. I am thankful that I have a great education, great jobs, good friends, family, and a passion for teaching and life coaching. However, after each great milestone that I've accomplished in my journey, my sub-conscious would seem to take over and come between my victories and blessings by always reflecting this negative thought, "If only I had done this when I was younger … I would been much further than I am today" Once that got into my head, my joy turned into sadness and disappointment because it took me so long to complete a task that I thought should have been done in my younger years. I began to meditate on how much time I had wasted, and thinking of the even longer list of things I had yet to accomplish, but could have gotten done due to the excuses in my life that I permitted to hold me back.

Looking back, I understand that my life could have taken many turns, and I am thankful for the opportunities that God has provided me with. I know that I could have done things at a younger age and could be a lot further than I am in my journey now. The fact is, life began for me at a later age. I do not regret that. I realize that God had a plan for me (in all of His wisdom) and had me, excel at a later age to write this book and to help others excel and move forward when they felt "stuck" in life.

Sometimes we get "stuck" in negative thinking which prevents us from doing what our heart desires and what the Lord commands us to do with our lives. We make excuses and blame others for our downfalls when things do not go the way we would like for them to go. This is how the "If" syndrome begins to take shape.

I had 10 big "If's" in my life that I thought held me back. Those ten were:

If only I was smart enough …
If only I was big enough …
If only I had worked harder …
If only I would have been there on time …
If only I could get a better job …
If only I had good looks like my brothers …
If only I was born into a rich family …
If only people could understand me …
If only I could be like that person …
If only I didn't have to do this by myself …

These ten "If's" took control of my life because I'd let this small word, "if" conditioned me by placing fear and doubt within myself and my capabilities of what I could do and what I have been told I am capable of doing. Some of those fears and doubts came from the environment.

I confess that I wasn't as positive back then as I am today. I'd been told by society and the haters of the world that a young, African-American male living in the urban area will rarely get the opportunity to move up in the world because of their backgrounds and their environment. I remember being told as a child that only the whites have the power to make things happen because they had the money and the influence. When I heard that, it made me start questioning my worth as a black young person growing up. I then began the "If" phase of my journey:

"What if this is true?
What if I do all of this hard work and it doesn't pay off?
If I don't have a chance now, why should I work for the future?"

I'd even had this crazy thought as a child that maybe I was being punished for being black. In my thinking (at that time), there's wasn't a chance on this earth, that I was going to be successful knowing what I had been told. So why should I work so hard if I am not going to get anywhere in life?

I must confess that I was ashamed during that period in my life because even though my parents raised us to be proud of who and what we were, I couldn't help but believe what we had been told of what society had expressed and brainwashed us to think about being black. It's not that I didn't believe my parents. However, the way they struggled to make ends meet and to see my father break down into tears when he felt his world and family crumbling around him because his check didn't cover enough for the bills, and not have enough to feed his family, made me believe that maybe society may had been right and I had to come to grips with that.

Well, it wasn't about being black at all. It was about the "If's" getting in the way of me being the best that I could be.

As an adult, I had still carried some of those "If's" in my life. It seemed as though "If" had been taken to another level. The "if's" become more defined and even more life challenging as I went through my journey. My thoughts were starting to effect the lives of those I loved the most. My "if" list from my younger years started effecting my mental and physical life. I'd realized I was in trouble when my thoughts were expressed only through the phrases using the word "if":

If I had only listened to my mother and father … I could have …
If I had only been a better student … I could have …
If only I didn't have children … I could be …
If only I had a better job … I would …
If only I made more money … I could …

I had come to realize in my adult life that the "if's" had taken over my complete being and I no longer felt like I was succeeding in anything. I only saw myself as just "getting things done." Once

I got the "chore" done, I would just check it off and move on to the next phase of what I had to do to keep it moving. There was no substance in my life. There was no meaning behind what I did. I would focus only on the stressors of my life. I would just live for my parents, my sons, my niece, and whoever needed me at the time. I was just existing to do for others. It felt as though as if I was just put here on Earth to take care of everyone else and to hell with my vision and purpose. My biggest "if" then became, ***"What if I could just walk away from all of this?"*** That question was the changing factor that changed my life forever. That "if" question was the "Be careful what you ask for" question that made me face my fears and doubts. God taught me a lesson that changed the way I saw the word "if." From that last "if" question that changed my life, I would never let the word "if" dominate my life ever again. This was a major turning point in my life to being the best that I could be.

I've never walked away from anything or anyone that I have been responsible for. However, be careful what you ask for. Even though I did not walk away, there have been a few special people in my life that I'd cherished the most were taken away from me and literally walked out of my life. The one person I will talk about is the one whom I've lived for the most … Momma. On the day my mother died, we had spent the whole day together. Little did I know that she was preparing me to walk out of my life for good (at least on Earth) It was as if Momma knew what was going on in my heart because the very last conversation we had was that she didn't want to be a burden to me and she wanted me to stop fussing over her and start enjoying my life. I told her that all that she has done for me in my life and how she took care of all of us, there is no way I would ever stop taking care of her. It was at that moment she told me that she was ready to see "KP" (my father) again. I told her that one day she will see him again. I just didn't know it would be later on that evening. The biggest "if" that changed my total life around was when I found myself alone in the world without "Momma." She left me, knowing that God had a plan for me. I didn't know that my life would be challenged in such a way that it would enhance my life making me becoming the best that I could be.

The thing I learned most from the word "if" is that this little word with such impact can keep you back and prolong you from doing what you need to do to succeed in your life and become the best you can be. I would like to see if I can help you help yourself be the best you can be by identifying the "If's" in your life. Do you still carry some of those "if's" in your life today? Let's see what the "if's" are in your life.

As an exercise that I use in my life coaching sessions, I would like for you to complete the following 5 sentences. Please take your time to think these sentences through and be honest with yourself.

1. If I could had only

   _____ ,

   I would have _____

   _____

2. If I could had only

   _____

   _____

   I would have

   _____

   _____

3. If only I could have

   _____

   _____

I would have

_____

_____

So, how did you do? Were you able to identify with any of the sentences you've completed? Every one of us has (at some point), used the phrase, "If only," "What if" or "If I." Most of the time, we use the word "if" in the negative sense because of the "lack of" or the "need to desire something" that is beyond your control. How did you use your "if" sentences? Did you use them in the negative sense as in regret? If you have, you are not alone. Even if you have used one in the negative sense, you are not alone. The word "if" brings many types of hurt, pain, and all types of memories that we wish we could forget. An example of this type of "if" is when we go through our lives regretting things and thinking back on what could have been, what we could have done better or what could have prevented this. So, in an attempt to make the pain "go away" or remove that pain or hurt from our physical and mental being, we transfer that pain and conflict you are experiencing onto someone else. Below are 15 phrases using the words "If only" I have created different sentence scenarios to show you how easy we can get caught up in the "if" syndrome. How many of you can relate to any of these phrases?

Once you have read the phrase, circle whether you "said it to someone" or "If this phrase was ever said to you." Try to be as honest and open as you can.

1. If only I (you) were more responsible.
   I've said it It was said to "me

2. If only I (you) were man enough.
   I've said it It was said to "me

3. If only I (you) had more money
    I've said it It was said to "me

4. If only I (you) were taller.
    I've said it It was said to "me

5. If only I (you) were better.
    I've said it It was said to "me

6. If only I could have listened to (my) your mother.
    I've said it It was said to "me

7. If only I could have listened to (my) your father.
    I've said it It was said to "me

8. If only I (you) could have been a better mother.
    I've said it It was said to "me

9. If only I (you) could have been a better father.
    I've said it It was said to "me

10. If only I (you) could have done things differently
    I've said it It was said to "me

11. If only I (you) didn't have children.
    I've said it It was said to "me

12. If only I (you) wanted children.
    I've said it It was said to "me

13. If only I (you) were more educated.
    I've said it It was said to "me

14. If only I (you) had finished school.
    I've said it It was said to "me

15. If only I (you) could have waited
I've said it It was said to "me

How did you do? If you checked off 3 or more on either sides of the check off lists, then you should continue to read on to get some solutions and how to change those negative "if's" and start rebuilding your focus. I believe that we are always in need of some type of repair, whether it is physically, mentally, emotionally and physically. I also believe that all of us have been effected by the "if" syndrome and still have some lasting effects from it. From someone who has experience his full share of "if" experiences, I would like to suggest a few tips regarding the "if" syndrome and getting past it.

If you are really serious about getting the most out of life and being the best you can be, let's start with the simple strategies.

DEAL WITH THE REAL ISSUE: If you have been hurt, or feel that you have been "broken" by people and things, know that you are in need of repair and you need to ***deal with the issue, and not how you feel about the issue.*** Now, I will explain in detail and guide you through the process. However, you will need to actually get a pen and paper if you really want to consider being the best you can be.

These are the questions that you need to answer:

Who was the person who did or said something that hurt you?
Actually saying (or) writing the person's name is very helpful. When we get mad or upset, we tend to want to block out that person's name and visual from our memory. Sometimes you do more harm than good when you try to create such tactics that will eventually never go away just by blocking out the memory of the person or just staying silent. As a safe tip to remember: The more you try to block the memory out, more visuals and memories come into play.

What did the person do or say that hurt you?

Sometimes it is good to write down exactly what the person said. If you can remember what the person said exactly, then there is credibility that what that person did or said actually affected you in a way that needs to be addressed. Know that **you do not have to go to the person directly**. Write it down. It's about journalizing emotions and getting to the heart of what the real issue is. In my sessions, I use different types of venues to express the thoughts and put them out there so that it's visual and they can connect the emotion with the writing on the wall.

By writing it down, you are validating your pain. You are using your writing utensil as a tool to get to the heart of what the person said. Now, if you really can't remember what the person said … WHY ARE YOU HOLDING THAT HURT? Anything not worth remembering is not worth carrying a grudge for. Part of the "if" factor is dealing with regrets. Also, consider the fact of what the person said? Were you hurt because there may be some truth to what the person is saying? This is truly the time for you to really think about this question. If you find that if there may be truth to what the person is saying, write down reasons on why you feel that the person is true about what they are saying. This has been an eye opener for many who have done this exercise. However, I don't have them stop here.

When did the person do or say something that hurt you?

If this person has said or did something over a year ago, WHY ARE YOU HOLDING THAT HURT? This is another "if" factor. "Time" in itself is lost in your emotion of hurt and pain. Once you lose this time, you will never get it back. This is where many big "If's" come in. Remember the phrase, "If I only had more time?" If it has been over a month, ask yourself … "Is it really worth holding a grudge and losing precious time behind it?"

Where did the person do or say something that hurt you?

Sometimes the "where" can make the difference in a person's mind. When writing things out, be clear and to the point. Ask yourself did the location where it happened make a difference. Did it happen in front of a group? Did the person say or do it just in front of you only? Was it a place where it holds good or bad memories for you? When journalizing your thoughts, keep in mind, every detail uncovers a piece of a puzzle. A location could hold a lot of feelings as well and take you back to a time and place where you could recollect regret.

Why did the person do or say something that hurt you?

This may be a good section because this is another area where the "AHA" moment comes into play. Once you start writing down the why to why you believe this person hurt you, you may discover a whole lot more to the story. Once you have written your thoughts out, read it back to yourself. If you can answer why to why you think that particular person hurt you, without involving yourself in the equation, then you may have justification and credibility in your actions for feeling the way you do. However, in the many exercises I have done with the many groups, there really hasn't been a time that I can remember where the actual person who was hurt from what was said, never was out of the picture completely. Once they actually wrote down the complete incident, there is a moment of silence and then regret because now they finally realize this whole incident may have been a miscommunication. Now think about the time wasted and energy spent on miscommunication.

How did the person do or say something that hurt you?

Now, even the "how" can be involved in the "if" syndrome because many people catch hurt feelings just by the way a statement sounds and how a person presents the statements to another person. However, you would need to ask yourself, "Should how the person say something to me make a difference in the way I feel?" Once you answer this question, you will know for sure whether or not this whole incident was worth it.

Maybe there is an incident you would like to go back over and see whether or not you regretted something for no reason at all. This would be a good time to practice journalizing an old wound you may still be going through. Anytime will be a good time to practice on bettering yourself. I will set up the questions for you and you can write in your book. Once you have written it out, read it back to yourself. Read it out loud so you can hear yourself. See if writing things out, helped you to minimize your regrets and opened up a new direction for you to go.

JOURNAL ENTRY

Who was the person who did or said something that hurt you?

_____

_____

What did the person do or said something that hurt you?

_____

_____

_____

_____

_____

_____

When did the person do or say something that hurt you?

_____

_____

_____

_____

_____

Where did the person do or say something that hurt you?

Why did the person do or say something that hurt you?

How did the person do or say something that hurt you?

---

1. One of the things that I would like for you to take with you from reading this book is when dealing with the word "if," there is also a greater side to this word. The word "if" can anticipate the agreement of a supported intention. This can generate the positive "if" factor by preceding positive antidotes in order to embrace the positive side of communication, enhancing and self-building of one's relationship and self. That is why I believe this word to be one of the deadliest words in our efforts to be the

best we can be ... It challenges us from both ends. Here are some examples you can use to start building up your positive communication skills that leads to self-worth. Complete these sentences with positive statements to practice building up positive momentum:

2. "If at any time I could do something good for myself, it would be

_____

_____ ,,

3. "If I listen carefully to the voice of the Lord, I believe that I can

_____

_____ ,,

4. "If I can be of help to someone, I would

_____

_____ ,,

From the biblical standpoint, we have many positive antidotes, using the "if "statement that assures us of a great life (as long as we believe it and receive it).

"If my people which are called by My name, shall humble themselves, and pray, and seek my face, and turn from their wicked ways, then will I hear from Heaven, and will forgive their sin, and will heal their land." (II Chronicles 7: 14).

"If I may but touch the hem of his garment I shall be made whole (Matthew 9:21)

"If ye be risen with Christ, speak those things which are above, where Christ is seated at the right hand of God." (Col. 3:1)

"And I, if I am lifted up from the earth I will draw all men unto Me." (John 12: 32)

So how do we sum up the "If" word? Let's start off with this :
1. When using the word "if," be aware of how you use it? Ask yourself whether you are using it in the positive or negative sense. For example;
Are you using "if" in the positive sense ... "If you will, please let me help you." vs. the negative sense ... "If he would have started sooner, he would have been finished by now."
Positive: "If you'd come this way, I will be more than happy to help you."
Negative:" If only you would have worked harder, you would have been as smart as them also."
It's all about the way we say things ... the delivery in how we talk to people that can make the difference in someone's life. What is even more ironic is the difference it would make in your own life if you would watch how you use the word "if" dealing with your own life. Despite what society says ... words do hurt. Sometimes, you can find yourself talking and putting yourself down just by using a small word such as "if" in a conversation to make an excuse for why you haven't accomplished the things you wanted to do in life. Just imagine how much of a change you can make in your own life just by changing the small words that causes such big problems.
Just make sure that if we are going to use the word "if," keep it positive. Keep it limited. Yes, keep it limited. The less you, use the word "if," the less chance you have of becoming negative and the better your chances are of not making a statement that you would regret later on in your journey called life.

"Can a woman forget her nursing child, that she should have no compassion on the son of her womb? Even these may forget, yet I will not forget you."

Isaiah 49:15

I sometimes forget that God has overlooked and forgiven me for the many wrongs that I may have done. So I should not forget to forgive others by forgetting the hurt from the past and moving forward. "It takes a believer to forget the hurt and pain that has been put on them by others and remember Christ. It takes a non-believer to forget that Christ exists in those times and live with the hurt and the pain"

Dr. Thomas L. Page

"FORGET"

There is really no type of script for this word. There is no safety net to cushion the fall for the word "*forget.*" There is no type of research that I am going to offer you to give validity to what I am writing. What I am going to write about is strictly from my experience on the art of *forgetting.* If you believe that the word "forgiveness" was a deadly word, then I would tend to think that the word "*forget*" is even a deadlier word that prevents us from being the best we can be.

How many times have we ever wanted to forget about something, but just couldn't? There were many nights where you lost sleep over an issue you wanted to forget about. I am sure that there were situations in our lives that we would've loved to forget and move on with. However, for some reason or another your pride and conscious kept eating at you. For some of you, it may have even affected you in such a way that you became physically ill and had to seek medical help.

I have learned from the many experiences of my life that to *forget* is a necessary part of the forgiveness process in order to begin the healing process.

I remember the many times I would really get sick and end up in a fetal position from those who have hurt me so bad. There were some days that I thought the hurt would never end. There were a few situations in particular where a couple of people who meant (and still does) everything in the world to me walked out of my life … some with no explanation. I kept going back to these people in order to find the reasons for just walking out of my life and not caring enough to tell me. I guess with people you really don't have a connection with, it wouldn't have bothered me so much. However, when someone you cared for and loved throughout your lifetime mistreats you and then turn their back on you, the hurt intensifies and is pretty much unbearable at the time.

Now you are probably wondering how did I not only forgive, but forget about this hurt that was put on me and moved on. Well there is really no great secret on how I did it. There was no mystery behind it. The key factor in all of this is that I never forgot. The key to forgetting is not pretending or believing that the hurt and pain that I went through didn't exist. Forgetting for me was not to recall the hurt and the pain I felt during those times and making a conscious choice on not to dwell on the person or situation behind the pain it caused me. This allowed me to move on to a place of peace and reconciliation with myself. It was not an easy task at first. It took a while to practice the art of forgetting in that way. I am a better person for it now and I thank God for the favor he has given me to teach others how to do the same.

I have been asked many times how does one go beyond past hurts and move on with their lives. In one of my life coaching sessions, I found myself in a situation where a young woman was abused and wanted to learn how to forgive her abusive boyfriend, forget the situation and start afresh with him, again. The woman was in such an emotional turmoil from this situation because there were still old, but visible marks still left on her arms from the past abuse. She talked about some of the abuse in detail, even down to what they were both wearing when the abuse took place. She was out of the situation temporarily, and living with family members. However, no matter how she wanted to forget about him and the past life that led her to this point, she couldn't stop thinking about the good life she had with him in the past, yet reliving the nightmares from the present abuse. In one particular session, she became so outraged and angry that she couldn't stop crying. The team members tried to rally around her to embrace and console her. I had everyone step back and let her go through the pain she was going through. It took about 10 minutes for her to compose herself. I did not want anyone to validate that she was hurting. I wanted this young woman to acknowledge the hurt she has gone through and is still going through. I wanted her to feel being angry at him, as well as herself. She even confessed to being worthless and powerless over this whole situation. I wanted her to go through all of that in the circle. By going through the emotions, you are finally getting the break though that one needs to move on to the next step.

Once this young woman finally able to compose herself and get through the emotional release to move forward, I then began to bring her to her truth. I asked her the following questions that changed her life forever:

1. When do you feel worthless?
2. Are you always feel rejection and hurt around this person?
3. Are you still familiarizing yourself with this person?
4. What is the attraction that is keeping you in this situation?

5. Is it worth your self-respect and dignity to stay connected with this person?
6. Are you strong enough to release yourself from this person?

The last question that I asked was a wake-up call for this young woman. As I was asking the last question to this young woman she asked me, "What did you mean, am I strong enough?" Within seconds, the "AHA "moment came into effect and she admitted to the group as well as herself that she had let someone control her life and that had to change. The blessing of all of this is that she is no longer with this young man and she is doing well and making great strides in becoming the best she can be.

For situations like this young woman, and those situations that you may find yourself in when it comes to wanting to forgive and especially *forget,* know that it is not an easy quick fix and then we move on with life. To *forget is a process,* just like forgiveness.

Through my own personal journey of forgetting, I have learned three major things that I continue to live by:

1. Surrender the need to understand the reason for our pain.
2. We have a CHOICE to forget
3. True forgetting means that there is true forgiveness.

There used to be a time in my life when I would ask God, "Why is this happening to me? I am a good person. I follow your laws and try to be the best I can be to all people. So, why are you allowing this to happen to me?" After a while, I would think that God was really getting tired of me asking that question. However, the fact that He never gave up on me was a testimony in itself and there was a lesson for me to be learned. Until I finally realized that I had to deal with the fact that I may never understand the reason(s) for the pain I am going through, I would continually finding myself in this constant battle with myself and will continue to struggle with the issue of forgetting.

The reality when the word "forget" became the AHA moment for me was when a person I truly loved, cared for and nurtured became estranged from me. The reason is still unknown to this day. It has been a while now since that incident happened. However, my emotions and my heart would always take me down the path of searching for the "why" in all of this. As someone who believe in not giving up on relationships that matter, I kept trying to connect and trying to talk and get a chance to sit with them if only to answer the question "why." They never wanted to make any type of contact with me. However, I kept focusing on trying to get answers because how could someone that I cared about so much do something like this to me without an explanation or reason. It wasn't until that moment when I caught up with them and asked if we could finally sit down and talk about what was going on. I heard the words that would change my life forever and taught me the true meaning to "forget." I was told to, "Stay the f@#! out of my life." That was the nail that punctured my heart, my ego, my soul and spirit. It was also the reality that I needed to start the process to "forget" this situation, this relationship and move on with my next phase of life. Even though I will never forget them in my heart, I realized that I couldn't control people or their lives. The only control that I had was over me. From that moment on, I'd embraced the fact that things happen for a reason … however, it is not my reason to know, but only to trust in God, His plan for me and learn from experience.

Now as I stated before, it is not an easy task to "forget." There were times when I thought of things that would attempt to bring me back to a road I did not want to go back down. The littlest things would almost set me back: The activities we would do together; the long nights going through emotional meltdowns and self-esteem issues; cooking their favorite foods and eating until we got full, weekly "dvd" nights and always, daily "I love you" affirmations and devotions. Once I honed the skills of forgiving and forgetting, along with a lot of prayer and practice, I was able to **"stop"** (whatever thought that was about to get into my head) … **"think"** (of what I am doing and about to do) and **"recite"** (as a constant reminder to myself), *"Let go of the past. It is not for me to understand the reason for my pain … However, only God knows the answer and I can live with that."*

Now, throughout this process to "forget," you must remember that you have a choice in the matter. Sometimes it's all about the choices we make that will decide if you will succeed or fail.

Throughout the above journey, I'd also come to realize that the choices I made, not only affected me emotionally. I'd notice that during that period I was losing weight, not eating, always worrying and it took a toll on my physical body. This situation caused me to doubt myself and my belief in the God that I served which affected me spiritually. It also affected me mentally. All of this came about from the choices that I made and accepted (at the time). Of course, things have definitely changed and I am a much better person for it.

I think that I have given a great example and steps on how to truly "forget." If you still are a little unsure if you can learn and master the art of forgetting, look at little children. Watch how they play and interact with each other. They can definitely teach us a lesson on how to *forget*. If you watch children, they are arguing one moment and then playing with each other the next. I would watch children fighting over building blocks and would fight for the ownership of the red building block. Once they would argue and fight, an adult would step in, make them apologize and shake hands. Once that process was over, they were up and running hand in hand, going back to having fun together. I would imagine if life was really that simple, we would all remain children and live a stress free life. Well, I am sorry to disappoint you … but life is not that … especially when learning to "forget."

As part of practicing the art of learning how to "forget" those things that holds us back from being the best that we can be, I would like to suggest an exercise that would start you on the way to at least thinking more positive and ready to make that change you would desire to be a better "you."

As part of my daily ritual and devotions, I name one affirmation a day on why I should always be happy. I would say in the mirror … "Today's reason why I am happy is because: "I am blessed beyond measure." This affirmation keeps me grounded and keeps me mindful of the things that I need to stay focused on. By staying focused on the positive affirmations, I seem to "forget" of those things that took control of my past life and keep me on a path moving forward to being the best that I can be.

I would like for you to work on your skills at "forgetting" Before you can get to the point where I am in my journey, let's take a look at an exercise in learning how to "*forget.*" I would like for you to practice by complete the following exercise by filling in the following statements (Remember to be as truthful as you can):

Situations in my life that are beyond my control but won't let me forget (I will start it off for you):

a.   Cheating on your partner (spouse)

b.   _____

c.   _____

d.   _____

e.   _____

Situations in my life that are beyond my control that I should forget:

a.   People talking negative about me.

b.   _____

c.   _____

d.   _____

e.   _____

Situations in my life that are within my control that I will forget:

a. The anger that I am holding over this person who hurt me.

b. _____

c. _____

d. _____

e. _____

Notice the last part of your exercise. It stated, "*Situations in my life that are within my control ...*" So I hope that you picked up on that phrase. That means you have control of your life in the areas that could matter most for you. This may be a pivotal moment for some of your right now. So take a moment to reflect what was just said. If you have some type of control in your life (in which we all do), you have the control to "forget" about situations that are beyond your control and can do it in a way that change the way you see your life in the "here and now."

Maybe at this point, you need to feel like you need to have more control of your own life and start to "forget" those things and people that have controlled your life for so long. Maybe you are feeling that now is the time to take back your life but don't really know how or where to start. Sometimes it is a slow process and you may have to take baby steps to get there. Let's start the process now.

One way to start the process on how to "forget" those things that prevents you from moving forward, is to see what you do have control over. Below, I have put down a starter list of things that you should have control of right now. Check off the ones that pertain to you and see if these are active now in your life. Be honest. Be truthful. This will be a starting point on how you can start taking back control by completing the items that you did not and find hard to check off. I would think that some of these may hit home for you and you are using them in your life today. Some of these items you may not have even tried yet. So, let's start checking off those items that you have control over and using them in your life right now:

AT THIS MOMENT IN TIME, I CAN CONTROL

_____ How many times I smiled today

_____ How much effort I put in at work

_____ Your level of honesty

_____ How well you prepare

_____ How I catch my thoughts before they become emotional reactions

_____ How often I say "Thank you"

_____ Whether or not someone gives me the benefit of the doubt

_____ How I interpret situations

_____ Whether or not I compete with people around you

_____ How often I notice or appreciate small acts of kindness

_____ Whether I listen when someone is talking

_____ Whether I wait to talk

_____ Whether I walk away from a conversation

_____ How nice I am to myself in my head

_____ Whether I think positive or negative thoughts

_____ Whether or not I give without expectations

_____ The type of food I eat

_____ When I answer someone's question-or email-or call

_____ How much time I spend worrying

_____ How many new things I can try

_____ How much exercise I get

_____ How many times I swear in traffic

_____ Whether or not I plan for the weather

_____ How much time I spend trying to convince people I am right

_____ How often I think about my past

_____ How many positive or negative articles I read

_____ The attention I give to my loved ones when I see them

_____ How much I enjoy the things I have right now, even though they're not perfect

_____ Whether or not I say what is on my mind

_____ How clean or cluttered I keep my space

_____ What books I read

_____ How well I network at social events

_____ How deeply I breathe when I experience stress

_____ How many times I admit I don't know something

_____ How many times I learn something new

_____ How often I use my influence to help others instead of focusing on me

_____ Which commitments I keep and cancel

_____ How many risks I take

_____ How creative/innovative I am in my thinking

_____ How clear I am when I explain my thoughts

_____ Whether I formulate a new plan or act on my existing one

_____ How much information I share with people

_____ Whether I smoke or drink

_____ Whether or not I judge other people

_____ Whether you smell good or bad

_____ How much of what people say I believe

_____ How quickly I try again after I fail

_____ How many times I say, "I love you"

_____ How much rest I get at night

This book will not have any immediate remedies for you. However, this book can be a starting point in taking control of your life again. You may have felt that society, relationships, family and everyone has said something to hurt you along the way, by telling you what you are (aren't), what you can (cannot) do and minimizing your self-worth by deciding the type of person you are by their expectations. By the time you start going through the above list and enjoying the many controls that you now have available, you will find that the past has passed and you are now moving on to a new experiences and a new level in your life. Practice makes perfect.

Love is patient and kind; love does not envy or boast; it is not arrogant or rude. It does not insist on its own way; it is not irritable or resentful; it does not rejoice at wrongdoing, but rejoices with the truth. Love bears all things, believes all things, hopes all things, endures all things. Love never ends. As for prophecies, they will pass away; as for tongues, they will cease; as for knowledge, it will pass away.
1 Corinthians 13:4-8

Love....what Mom & Pop gave to me unconditionally. No better love than this on earth....except for the unconditional love from the Father above. Wow! Now I have all three from above shining their unconditional love on me to pass on to those I've raised, those I've met, and those I've yet to meet.
Dr. Thomas L. Page

"LOVE"

When you think of the word "love," what is your very first thought? Do you know the true meaning? By the time you finish reading this section of the book, you will realize why I chose "love" as the last of the seven deadliest words.

In my past understanding of the word "love," I had always meant it to be an action verb, a command required of us from God. Love was something that our parents taught us to do when it came to our brothers and sisters, especially when we were fighting or disagreed. I have to be honest. Love being unconditional (at first) didn't mean anything to me because I wasn't a parent, wasn't responsible for anyone else's life, and at the time, didn't really care about anything but surviving and meeting my needs. During that period, whenever I heard the word "love," it was in the context of this phrase, "If you love me, you would ..." It had nothing to do with being unconditional. As a matter of fact, it was always the opposite. There was always a conditional to whatever love I had received as an emerging adult. It seemed as though during my younger years, there was really no need for a true commitment that would cause me to make use of the term, "unconditional love."

The real, true, unconditional "love" came from my parents. Momma would exercise that unconditional love to not only her children, but for anyone who would come into our household. She would feed them, give them a roof over their head (if they needed it), and even clothed them (if they needed clothes}. She would listen and not judge. This woman was amazing. She was truly one that I would say that would represent unconditional love the way I understood it at its best.

It wasn't until I became a parent when I grasped the real concept of "unconditional love." As a matter of fact, one of my sons actually challenged my thought process when it came to the word "love." Every day before I would drop him off to school, I would give him a kiss on the forehead or cheek, and I would always tell him "I love you." One night during devotions, he asked me, "How much do you really love me?" I really didn't have to prepare for a question like that, especially coming from my 10 year old son. However, it did throw me off because how could someone so young ask such an adult question. It was as if I was talking to an old man. Before I answered that question, us and remembering what my father said to us. I remember my father saying to me that he would die for us ... that was how much he loved us. But at the end of the statement he would say ... "But don't test me ..." Even though it was funny to me at the time, I knew that he meant it. That is what I called unconditional and true love. I told my son the same thing (without the "test" part). I would lay down my life for him. Sometimes I don't think that when we talk about "love," we understand the true concept of what we are saying.

We throw the word "love" around like loose change. As someone who deals with clients who are suffering from the lack of love, I have come to realize a few things about the word "love."

1. Love can definitely be taken for granted.

During my "searching for love" and writing my dissertation, I will always remember some quotes that has stuck with me whenever I thought of the love I received in my life. One said, "Never trust a person that has let you down twice. One time was a warning, two times was a lesson … anything passed two times is simply taking advantage." If I could have just gotten a dollar every time someone would tell me, "If you loved me, you would …" I would not have to be writing this book. Now during that time, I would give in due to the fact that when I loved someone (of what I thought was real love), I wanted to be sincere in being true to my word and did what I could to please those I did say I loved. Looking back I could really kick myself in the pants. However, God had a plan for me. I just didn't know it then.

There was one more quote that I carried with me throughout my adult life. It said (paraphrasing it), "If you allow a person to make more withdrawals then deposits in your life, you will be out of balance and in the negative. Know when to close the account." I carried that quote with me everywhere I'd went after discovering how much I'd been taken advantage of, especially by some of the ones I loved and cared for the most. I would do all that I could and would go out of my way (for a long time) to show my unconditional love. At one point, I ended up being stiffed out of a substantial amount of money because "if I loved them … then I would do this for them." I had been drained out of the love and most of my material possessions. But the biggest and saddest part of all (that became a turning point) was that it was MY CHOICE. I LET THEM DO THIS TO ME.

It became apparent that the more I tried to help them, the more they demanded. When I wasn't able to fulfill their wants and desires, I still ended up as the bad one and I would be told that, "I knew you didn't really love them" because ..." You can fill the rest of that sentence with whatever you want because I am sure that you have heard this statement before in your journey. It has probably happened to you more than once. Can you remember a time when this happened to you? Do you remember what the circumstance(s) or thing was that would lead them to say, "If you love me, you would ...? If you can remember the circumstance(s), write them down (Go up to three circumstances):

1. _____
2. _____
3. _____

Whether it was over material things such as money, a loan or a car, or even doing simple tasks they could have done themselves, you were never the same in their eyes again because you didn't meet the full need of that person.

Some of the people I truly loved and cared about more than life itself used "love" against me. I am no longer the victim. Now, I only take it out and read it to myself when I find myself overwhelmed with the fear of someone taking advantage of me and using "love" as a tactic to get it. This was when the light came on for me. I realized that if I kept letting people drain me and take advantage of my love as a weakness, I was going to be worthless to myself. This was also a turning point for me where I found the meaning of what true "love" really meant.

I have come to the point that if I am truly going to advise you on my thoughts on the word "love" and how you can use this word to give your life full meaning and joy, I would really have to go the source where I receive all of my strength and wisdom from ... *the Bible.*

I Corinthians 13 (NIV) states:

> *13 If I speak in the tongues[a] of men or of angels, but do not have love, I am only a resounding gong or a clanging cymbal. ² If I have the gift of prophecy and can fathom all mysteries and all knowledge, and if I have a faith that can move mountains, but do not have love, I am nothing. ³ If I give all I possess to the poor and give over my body to hardship that I may boast, [b] but do not have love, I gain nothing.*

> *⁴ Love is patient, love is kind. It does not envy, it does not boast, it is not proud. ⁵ It does not dishonor others, it is not self-seeking, it is not easily angered, it keeps no record of wrongs. ⁶ Love does not delight in evil but rejoices with the truth. ⁷ It always protects, always trusts, always hopes, always perseveres.*

> *⁸ Love never fails. But where there are prophecies, they will cease; where there are tongues, they will be stilled; where there is knowledge, it will pass away. ⁹ For we know in part and we prophesy in part, ¹⁰ but when completeness comes, what is in part disappears. ¹¹ When I was a child, I talked like a child, I thought like a child, I reasoned like a child. When I became a man, I put the ways of childhood behind me. ¹² For now we see only a reflection as in a mirror; then we shall see face to face. Now I know in part; then I shall know fully, even as I am fully known.*

> *¹³ And now these three remain: faith, hope and love. But the greatest of these is love.*

Throughout my growing years, I would read this all of the time. We would study it, but it was just something we studied and it had no true meaning to it. After reading this as a saved adult, I began to truly value the meaning of the word "love." I also became nervous because of how powerful this word truly was. I'd always thought of myself as a loving person. However, I truly fell short of my interpretation and what I was supposed to do when it came to the actions and commands of "love." When I first looked at 1 Corinthians 13 (and really started researching its context), I noticed quite a few things that I have discovered and would like to share with you.

DID YOU KNOW?

Verses 1-3 is all based on the words "*if*" and "*but*" (remember reading about those two words?).

Verses 4-8a gives us a glimpse of what love "*is,*" "*is not,*" and "*always.*"

Verses 8b-10 guides us into things that we should (and need to) be aware of if we are going to truly "love." In this section, everything is based on the words "*where there are … they will/ is …*" This section seems to be giving us the heads up, a warning of things to come that we need to be prepared for if we are truly going to make the step to love someone. It is almost as if Christ is showing us (or giving us a glimpse of the possible consequences to these actions. I saw the word "tongues" and it truly scared me because of the way I have used (and some of you) tongue to hurt others (even out of love). Just knowing the consequences put me on notice and warned me (as well as you) of the things we should say as well as how to say it.

Verse 11 Christ gives us an example of how we should develop into that "love" He so wants us to have and experience.

Verse 12-13 Christ prepares us for the future through His benediction with the important things that is to remain in our lives and even the greatest thing … which is "love."

Now I am going to reveal the part that makes the word "love" so deadly. If we truly want our lives to have the meaning and purpose we desire and want, we must learn to truly understand what we need to do to obtain that "love." I hope that you are ready and willing to do what it takes. I am going to suggest to you some techniques that I have found to work and be very helpful.

If you really intend to "love," know the real action behind it. Love is "doing the impossible," acknowledging that love is a greater power that we can ever possess. It is greater than the gifts that we possess. Yes, the gift that we possess from God is temporary, whereas love is eternal. The gifts that we possess are to be used in our present lives, the "here and now." To be even more specific, we are to put this love to use between Jesus' first and second comings. His first coming has already taken place. So the time to start is now.

How many of us have fallen short of speaking in the tongues of men and of angels? How many of us have fallen short of giving the gift of prophecy and solving all mysteries and all knowledge? How many of us have fallen short of having (and keeping) that faith that can move mountains? How many of us have fallen short of giving to the poor and surrendering your bodies to the flame? To put in easier terms … How many of us have fallen short of giving of ourselves so much as to avoid being forcibly exposed for being dishonest and dishonored? Well, if you have fallen short to at least one of these thoughts, know that you have some work to do. You have not even gone past the first three verses of 1Corinthians 13, yet. That is something to take notice of in itself.

This is a big step for many of us to admit that we have fallen short of giving the love that we were instructed to give. What's even more evident to note is that we have fallen short in giving the love that we need to ourselves. In order to love others, you must learn to love yourself first. One of the key elements to understanding how to "love" the way you should understands the "love" you have been missing in your own lives. What does that entail? Let's take a look to see what you have been missing.

You may feel that you did not get the kind words of encouragement or the gift of God's promise from anyone who mattered in your life that equated love. For some of us, our knowledge of love came from the way of receiving structured discipline that equated love as a child and adolescent. We may not have liked the type of discipline we received as a child or adolescent. However, it was a sign to many of us that our parents cared enough to discipline us and keep us on the right path.

Love for you may have been the material gifts that I talked about earlier and you did not receive those material things that you thought equated love in your life. You may have felt that you have been given empty promises that you'd though equated to "love." I see many young people today who have been manipulated by their parents through material gifts, equating it to love. Instead of showing the right form of love through structured discipline, some were bribed into changing their behavior through material things, as if their child was an animal and they were getting a reward for doing tricks. This type of manipulated love was a reward for behaving the way you were supposed to behave (whether at home or in school). Showing love by teaching your children and adolescents about being responsible and knowing how to act does not receive material gifts. This is part of the development process towards maturity. I am not really sure where we (as parents) went wrong into thinking material gifts became the grounds for changing behaviors. The results from this has caused many families to become dysfunctional and when the time comes for our children and adolescents to go out into the "real world," they have now formed in the back of their minds that they are to receive rewards or material gifts for acting a certain way. The consequences equating material things with love have affected many families in a negative way. It has even destroyed our children by thinking you can buy "love."

You may feel that your faith has been tested over and over and over and over again and you failed at faith when it mattered the most. The faith that you thought you failed at was part of the "love" package that you felt no longer existed since you lost your faith.

Did any of these scenarios apply to you? List those items above that applied to you. There may be some other items that I may have missed that you would like to add to your list. Feel free to add those to see what you have been missing when it came to your interpretation of "love."

_____

_____

_____

_____

_____

_____

_____

There was no right or wrong answer. I wanted you to see for yourself (in black and white) what you felt was the "love" that you thought was missing out of your life. We all felt "love" slip away from us at some point in our lives. Some of you are still carrying that emptiness with you, which is hindering you from being the best you can be and giving the "love" back to others as part of our command from God. Know that you are ok. You are not alone in your thinking. We all have felt that lack of "love" in our lives that could have changed our lives for the better.

The great news is that it is not too late. No matter how many times you have fallen short in your life … no matter how many times your loved ones have given you grief and heartache, suffering, manipulation and sorrow, you are still here. You are still in the land of the living. You have been given another chance at true "love." All you have to do now is know what the real instructions for "love" are and learn how to love yourself again. By learning to love yourself, you can learn to love others the true way God intended us to love and be loved. Let's start with what "love" is.

Love is an action, a command from God that we should practice on a daily basis. Love is patient and kind. Just from these two words alone, I had failed miserably in the past. My patience had been very short and my interpretation of being kind was only an option if people were kind to me. The thing that I have learned about these two words is that they are an action that can be practiced daily and, in time would result in a better quality of life for myself. The same lesson can be learned by you.

Patience is one of the fruits of the spirit, a quality that Jesus, himself possessed. I can only imagine what it must have been like for Christ to show patience for the many sinners who challenged Him. However, I can see the beauty of His patience for those who believed in Him and received eternal life. How many times have we been challenged in our lives to show patience? I am so thankful that God never gave up on me for the many times I have lacked in patience. I wasn't really sure at first, how patience could change my life for the better. I'd always thought that patience was a virtue, moral goodness that was something we needed to keep our blood pressure down and something that was taught by our parents as a way of teaching us lessons and keeping us out of trouble. Now, knowing what I know, it is so much more.

What does the word "patient" mean to you? Before I reveal what I have learned about what "patient" is, write down your meaning of the word, "patience." Don't go looking for a dictionary or a thesaurus. Write the definition from your heart and spirit. Go off of your present experiences, what you define as "patient":

"Patient" is:

_____

_____

_____

_____

_____

_____

If you were someone such as me, you would have found yourself writing the definition of "patient" as "someone who does not complain" or someone who does not groan or offers any type of resistance. I am sure that we can give many examples of someone with a patient spirit. I can always revert back to someone like my mother or father. I could remember at least one situation where my "Pop" showed the extreme art of being patient. I'd always say that my "Pop" had the patience of Job. I remembered getting into a car accident and wrecking Pop's car. I'd thought I was going to get killed and had to pay for the damages. Instead, Pop would just ask me if I was alright. I told him I was fine and he just said the words, "OK," I'll take care of it. Now for me that was essence of being patient. But for some reason, I believed being "patient" was much more. Whenever I would say things like that to my sons whenever I tried to show the art of being patient to them, it wasn't quite the same way as when my mother or father said it to me. I'd get a knot in my stomach the size of a lemon and would grit my teeth as to cover up what I'd really feel and would want to say. I would even start sweating from the forehead at times when I tried to show patience.

Sometimes, being patient didn't work for me. It wasn't until the death of my "Pop" where I learned the true art of being patient. Having to watch my mother deal with the pain and loss of her husband of 55 years, and having to endure her discomfort and distress without complaining, I'd learned how to become compassionate and generous to my mother, gaining a great strength in experiencing self-control and humility through her grieving process. It was at the time that I realized it wasn't about me, but about the life of someone else who needed my "love." Also during that time, my son was going through a loss/separation process where there were many sleepless nights and long days where he needed to know that I was there with him all the way ... through anger ... through his rage ... through his pain ... and even through his ability to become accepting of his situation he found himself in. It was because of circumstances like these where being uncomfortable for somebody else other than you and refusing to complain gave me clarity on the meaning of being patient.

As far as being "kind," this is also a fruit of the spirit. However, with being kind, I had to get a clearer understanding for me to become the best I can be. I have discovered a couple of things about being "kind." I can see that Jesus himself showed his kindness to everyone ... even his enemies. I tried that one time and got so frustrated that I walked away and never looked back at the situation ... or at least I thought I did. It was funny, however, because where I thought I was getting away from the situation, it seemed as though God brought me back to a similar situation where I had to learn from it. I think back on the time being estranged from one of my sons, I kept thinking to myself, why should I exercise being kind to someone who was so ungrateful and nasty to me. I would over extend myself to him and showed him so much love and compassion. I would reach out to him and send letters and emails letting him know that I am there for him and the "door will always be open to him if he would like to talk." Sometimes I felt like I was doing this for nothing. It started playing on my emotions and almost had me questioning my faith in God and the promise He made to us ... never to leave us nor forsake us. God is awesome. He never left me. However, I almost lost my head for that moment and left Him. I knew God never left me. What made it even more amazing that I was going through the hurt that my son put me through, I was taught the value of being kind, even the adversity I was going through with my son. Little did I know that through all of this that I was going through with my son, remaining kind was necessary for my growth in being the best that I could be (for him as well as myself). I remained consistent in my trials and tribulations, knowing that "He causes the sun to rise on the evil and the good, and sends rain on the righteous and unrighteous" (Matthew 5:45). I also had to remember that in all of the pain that I was going through, my son was going through his own battle with his own personal pain and struggles in his life. I had to remember that Jesus commanded me to love him regardless of how bad I was treated by him. I had to be good to him and lend to him without expecting to get anything back. A light came on when I realized through my personal devotions that even Jesus was kind to the ungrateful and wicked. So, who was I to cast any type of judgment on my son or anyone else for that matter? Being a true believer of this knowledge, I have come to learn that being kind taught me about repentance. Being kind to others leads us to repentance.

If you want to truly be the best that you can be, you must be able to swallow a whole lot of pride and be able to accept the things you cannot change. You must be able to look past the hurt and rejection of those who have hurt you. You will need to look past the ignorance of those people in your life that ridicules and still talk about you. You must look past all of that, and still be kind to those you feel don't deserve your kindness. Be clear, this doesn't mean that you still take the abuse of this person. You can still be kind from a distance. As long as you remain kind to those who have hurt you, God will take care of the rest. All you need to do is continue to believe that He will keep his promise to you.

Can you name some people in your life that you find you need to go back and be kind to? Even after the fact? Do you have some unfinished business with some people in your life that seem to still have some type of control over you that you need to come full circle with? If so, list their name(s) and why you need to rectify situations with them. You may have more than one. Be specific on how they still have control over you and what you need to say to them to release that "hold" they have over you. Remember, in kindness, we will overcome any adversity.

_____

_____

_____

_____

_____

_____

Now let's see what love "is not" and "does not." When we read about "love" in Corinthians 13, it is very specific on what love is and is not. We are now going to highlight on the "is/have nots." Love does not: envy, boast, keep record of wrongs and does not delight in the evil. Love is not: proud, rude, self-seeking, nor is not easily angered. Well, I can list a number of the above that I have harbored for a long time. I think back about some of these things that love is not and how much I have been a part of these awful things. It took a while for some of these worldly sins to leave my system. Every now and again, I slip up on the "keep record of wrongs" and being "rude." However, I always make it a practice of going back and remembering the way I felt back then and the way I have overcome those wrongs and feeling great about myself now. I am at my best right now and I will not do anything to jeopardize this happiness that I have. So it was easy to stop those wrongs. If you would like to see where you are at in your walk with the "wrongs" and would like to get back on track at being the best you can be, complete the next exercise by checking off all that applies to your life right now. Be honest and true with yourself. The truth always brings about change:

Part 1: In my journey right now:

_____ I still become envious of others

_____ I still boast

_____ I still keep records of wrongs

_____ I still delight in evil

_____ I am still proud (don't ask for help)

_____ I still get rude with others

_____ I am still self-seeking (only looking out for myself)

_____ I am still easily angered

Part 2: Things I can do to avoid and change these wrongs I selected. Only complete those items that apply to you:

In order for me to become less envious of others, I can

_____

_____

_____

To keep from boasting about myself, I can

_____

_____

_____

To stop keeping records of the wrongs that others have done to me, I can

_____

_____

_____

To stop delighting in evil, I can

_____

_____

_____

To stop becoming so proud and acting like I don't need any one's help, I can

_____

_____

_____

To stop being rude to others, I can

_____

_____

_____

In order to stop always looking out for myself, I can

_____

_____

_____

To prevent from being easily angered, I can

_____

_____

_____

The thing that I love about this exercise is that you get a chance to read and acknowledge those weaknesses that you have and work on them if you are truly going to exercise "love" for yourself and for others.

In life coaching sessions, I do this exercise, along with many others to help those who need to understand where they may fall short and want to strengthen their skills in "love." If you believe that you are struggling in this area, don't pass up this exercise. It will truly help you create a promise to yourself and help you stick to it by catching yourself as you are caught in the act of doing it from here on end. It does work.

In Corinthians 13, there is a section that Jesus assures us of what love will "always" do. We can be assured that "love" will always protect, trusts, hopes and perseveres. Love will also rejoice in the truth and never fails. These are some strong statements and assurances. If this is our assurance from Jesus Christ, we should be happy all day long, 365 days, 24 hours a day, 7 days a week. However, it is not that simple. In order for us to get the reassurance that Jesus offers, we have to do what I would call the "APA Plan" … Acknowledge … Practice … Achieve.

I took each assurance that Jesus wrote about and use the "APA Plan" to reach that goal. For example:

God assures us that "love" always protect. So, in order for me to meet this goal for the week, I would do the following:

"Acknowledge" that I need help in this area. By acknowledging this fact, I would seek the resources needed to see what it means to "protect." I would then *"Practice"* by looking up the word "protect" to get its true meaning of the word. A dictionary would do fine at this point when seeking wisdom. I would, then, seek God's definition on what it meant when God assured us that "love always protect." through the "Word." That meant going into my private, devotional time with God, searching and reading scriptures that would assure me of this protection of love. From there, I would pray for God to implant in me that gift to pass on this message to others or share that same love of protection to others. This helped me to "Achieve" this fruit of the spirit by passing this good news to others, sharing this type of love that would change lives forever.

I would practice everything that pertained to the answers I had written down and stuck to the plan until I'd mastered the skill to "protect." Let's say that I didn't meet the goal for that week. I didn't get frustrated nor did I give up. I gave myself time to work on it. Sometimes it took more than one day, one week or even one month to complete this section. Once I was well into knowing the steps to take to reach this type of "love," I would go back, see what I could have done better and change my strategy. Sometimes changing the way we think means going back to the basics; asking God for help. Prayer works. That means spending more time alone with yourself ... talking to God, asking Him to change your focus by changing your heart and getting a better understanding. However, you must be opened to this type of understanding.

I did this exercise as a promise that I made to God and myself because I really wanted to master the art of "love" and to follow through with all of the exercises if I was going to be an effective life coach as well as the best that I could be. I had to really work hard at each entity because to "love" is the hardest thing that I had to stay committed to. There were so many obstacles and things to remember that I wasn't able to master it all at once. Just know that that key to love and knowing what love is all about. Also know that when I spent more time to myself conversing with God, things became clearer in my mind as to what was expected of me if I was to live the best life possible. When the change came, it was overwhelming, but not so much that I couldn't handle what God had in store for me. This was when I realized that "Love never fails."

God now demonstrates to us how this type of "love" that is promised to us will never fail. He made this promise to us that if we do our part by remain steadfast and unmovable in this "love" He so desires for us to have and pass along to others, He would do His part. Now who on Earth can give us these type of promises with a guarantee?

"Where there are prophecies, they will cease;
Where there are tongues, they will be stilled;
Where there is knowledge, it will pass away;
When perfection comes, the imperfect will disappear"

So no matter what storms come into our lives, we have the tools, resources and assurance to keep moving forward in making the best life possible for ourselves through love.

He now gives us further instructions on how we should maintain this powerful love that you now understand. God is encouraging us at this point … "For we know in part and we prophesy in part." Now that we know what we know, we can now go out and share this love to others, with the guarantee of receiving the true love that you seek for yourself.

Now the last part of "love" may challenge some of you. Because of your past and the way you grew up, you may have a hard time comprehending and understanding this part. However, I will help you through this process. If you are ever going to experience this love that you desire to be the best you can be, you must first experience being loved as a "child." When Jesus stated in Corinthians 13: 11: "When I was a child, I talked like a child; I thought like a child, I reasoned like a child. When I became a man, I put childish ways behind me." So of you may feel that as a child, you were never loved and the love that you received was through neglect, abuse or hurt. So, if you have felt this time of childhood, know that you may not have experienced the type of love that a child receives. However, take the time out of your busy schedule to watch a mother and/or father interact with their baby or child. They immerse their children in love. But what comes across even more that I would like for you to observe is the love that child gives back to the parent and the interaction that takes place. Watching that and looking at the interaction of unconditional love is something that you can obtain.

For someone who has never experienced love as a child, I want you to know that is not an excuse for you not receiving and giving the love you truly desire. In my life coaching class, I do an exercise where I take you on a journey going back to the childhood you'd wished you could have. I take everyone back to that specific time in their childhood to go back and re-create the childhood they've always wanted. The purpose of this exercise was to embrace and capture the feeling of being "loved." The success of this exercise is that people got the opportunity to feel that love they've always desired (if only for a moment). By capturing that love, they now realized that they could feel what love is and actually practice loving others and receiving that love … no matter what unfortunate circumstances happened in your past. It is never too late to receive and give that love that God desires for us to have. It's within your reach. All you have to do is ask … and it shall be given.

What now should become evident to you is the benediction of Jesus' final words to us to make sure that you don't forget what is important in fulfilling your life and making it the best it can be … "Now I know in part; then I shall know fully, even as I am fully known. And now these three remain: faith, hope and love. But the greatest of these is *love* (I Cor. 13:12b-13).

THE PICTURES ...

1. Success: The power to soar the height of heights ... making no boundaries for yourself.
2. Prayer: I go to a place where all is quiet and I humble myself ... just to spend time to talk with my God and Father. We all have that quiet place within us.
3. Forgive: To forgive is like the snow built around a fire. The inner self could be blazing with beauty, but our hurt and anger always surround that beauty with the coldness of the outside of us ... preventing us to move forward.
4. But: When we let the word, "but" take over our lives, we are like branches covered with snow ... frozen in time, can't seem to move either way ... we're stuck, paralyzed and can't seem to move forward with our lives.
5. If: If we keep basing our lives on the word "if", we will be like the forest that swallows us up, feeling lost and overwhelmed because everything looks the same. However, our lives will be unclear, just like directions trying to get out of the forest ... always wondering where it could lead and never knowing where it (our lives) goes.
6. Forget: Sometimes we forget about the things that matter the most in our lives. It comes and it goes as a beautiful Lily. Yet, sometimes in our lives we forget what the true

beauty and the blessings are until it has passed us by and we forget what it looked like.

Love: Love for me will always be what God has given me all of my life … the love, comfort, joy, peace and blessings of beautiful parents. Sometimes it doesn't have to be a parent to feel love. When you love yourself and love God above all others, the love will find you.

I took these pictures throughout my lifetime and I cherish and capture those moments as a memory of the seven words in my life that has taken me through my valleys, yet has elevated me to a place where only God can enter. For where there is God, the Spirit that leads us … we have divine grace and peace like no other. This is my journey. It began with God and will end with God.

TRUE DIRECTIONS

An affiliate of Tarcher Perigee

OUR MISSION

Tarcher Perigee's mission has always been to publish books that contain great ideas. Why? Because:

GREAT LIVES BEGIN WITH GREAT IDEAS

At Tarcher Perigee, we recognize that many talented authors, speakers, educators, and thought-leaders share this mission and deserve to be published – many more than Tarcher Perigee can reasonably publish ourselves. True Directions is ideal for authors and books that increase awareness, raise consciousness, and inspire others to live their ideals and passions.

Like Tarcher Perigee, True Directions books are designed to do three things: inspire, inform, and motivate.

Thus, True Directions is an ideal way for these important voices to bring their messages of hope, healing, and help to the world.

Every book published by True Directions– whether it is non-fiction, memoir, novel, poetry or children's book – continues Tarcher Perigee's mission to publish works that bring positive change in the world. We invite you to join our mission.

For more information, see the True Directions website:

www.iUniverse.com/TrueDirections/SignUp

Be a part of Tarcher Perigee's community to bring positive change in this world! See exclusive author videos, discover new and exciting books, learn about upcoming events, connect with author blogs and websites, and more! www.tarcherbooks.com

TRUE DIRECTIONS

AN AFFILIATE OF TARCHER PERIGEE